The Meaning and Beauty of the Artificial

D. E. Harding

I0152517

The Meaning and Beauty of the Artificial

Published by The Shollond Trust
87B Cazenove Road
London N16 6BB
England

headexchange@gn.apc.org
www.headless.org

The Shollond Trust is a UK charity, reg. no 1059551
Copyright © The Shollond Trust 2021
Design and layout by rangsgraphics.com
ISBN 978-1-908774-98-9

The Shollond Trust

London

FOREWORD

Douglas Harding (1909–2007) was a British philosopher and mystic who worked out a modern map of our place in the universe. Then he showed how this scientifically verifiable map dovetails with the essential truth at the heart of the world's chief religions. Harding also invented experiments that enable anyone to test the validity of this map and at the same time experience the Reality that all great mystics celebrate—the Self that is nearer to you than your own heart.

Probably Harding is best known for *On Having No Head,* published in 1961. This easy-to-read book introduces the 'headless' experience, then explores its meaning and practical application. His greatest philosophical work is *The Hierarchy of Heaven and Earth,* published in 1952. This is a vast, deep, wide and magnificent masterpiece, a little-known work of genius far ahead of its time.

The Meaning and Beauty of the Artificial was Harding's first work of non-fiction, written in his 20s. At its heart is the idea that there is no absolute dividing line between the natural and the artificial. Though your body is part of 'nature' and the tool you pick up is an 'artifice', where is the dividing line between them? Are not tools extensions of your body, thereby extending your life into the society around you? Is there really an absolute boundary between yourself and the world?

Harding raises these philosophical questions but then quickly grabs you by the hand to take you on safari, on a well-informed and fascinating tour of the behaviour of animals, insects and birds that

i

use tools in astonishing ways, or live in societies where individuals are in effect organs of the communal body. But this safari also moves to the human world, opening your eyes to seeing 'man and machine' in a new way. And throughout this wide-ranging trip, from the study of primitive organisms to complex societies, from the principles underlying the design, function and evolution of tools to the philosophy of identity, Harding demonstrates a deep understanding and encyclopaedic knowledge. All of which is conveyed in a friendly clear style. Harding was already developing into a good writer.

Harding began *The Meaning and Beauty of the Artificial* in 1932. He had recently qualified as an architect and was working in the City of London. (For a Mr. Low, for £3 a week!) But what was it that inspired Harding to spend many a lunch hour studying cytology, sociology, philosophy and other subjects in the library? Probably there were several things going on. Two years before, Harding had formally rejected the religion of his childhood, the fundamentalist Christian faith of his father. But though he could not accept its narrow and often fantastic beliefs, that religion had given him the feeling he belonged, that he had a special place in the world, and that the Power behind the world loved him. In that cosmos he found himself within a context of meaning bigger (and better) than himself. So although Harding had rejected that pre-scientific world-view when he was 21, he still needed a meaningful (and loving) frame of reference. But it had to be credible. Which led him to using scientific methods to question and explore what it was to be human. Looking inside, biology revealed he was made of cells. Which are living animals.

How could he, Harding wondered, as an 'individual', be made up of millions of smaller 'individuals'? What did their presence imply for the notion of his 'self'? What was his relationship to these beings and their relationship to him? Or simply, who was he?

Then, stepping back from the close view, Harding looked into his relationship with the world around him and realised that he as an 'individual' existed like a cell in the greater body of society. It was growing clearer that however he looked at himself, he couldn't limit himself to 'Douglas Harding'. Crossing over the boundary between the self and the not-self he began to glimpse new vistas of tremendous depth and meaning. Having the courage to rely on scientific evidence rather than on the 'revealed truth' of Scripture was paying dividends. He was starting to discover a world profoundly different from the conventional world, a richly-layered, hierarchically-organised cosmos that pointed to the rapprochement with Reality his heart yearned for.

But as well as searching for meaning, for a place in the world, for a 'credible' God, Harding wanted to make a mark on the world. His mark. He was an ambitious young man. And though at school he was good at art, and though he came top in the Royal Institute of British Architecture exams, his passion was ideas and words and his dream was to be a thinker, a writer. (Dickens was one of his heroes.) But Harding did not just dream, he got down to serious work. Within three years he had the first draft of *The Meaning and Beauty of the Artificial* completed. Which meant that as well as working as an architect he had the determination, self-discipline and creative talent to think deeply, conduct extensive research, organise his ideas, presumably write and re-write one draft after another, and all without any external help or deadline. It came from within him. He must have spent many hours working alone whilst his contemporaries did all the things normal young people did in the mid-1930s. In 1935 Harding was only 26 and unknown as a writer but he believed in himself and his ideas enough to send his manuscript to Julian Huxley, brother of the novelist Aldous Huxley. Huxley was a leading evolutionary biologist and the secretary of the Zoological Society of London and senior to Harding by 22 years. But he liked what he read and offered to write a foreword. Harding went to meet him at the Society. Now there's a self-confident young man determined to go places!

As it happened, Huxley didn't write a foreword. This was partly because Harding had other ideas. Lots of them. So the book continued to evolve and meanwhile Harding moved on from the idea of the foreword by Huxley. But other things were happening too. Harding got married, visited Russia to observe how communism was working out there (badly!), applied for and got a job in India, sailed to Calcutta in 1937 with his wife, then started a family there. In his architectural job he led a team of about 30 draughts-men and -women. In his spare time in India he wrote a detective novel, became the cartoonist for a newspaper, gave talks on the radio and took up photography. He was firing on all cylinders. Yet still there bubbled away, beneath all this activity, the deep and insistent need to find meaning. So he continued to think, to read, to write, and *The Meaning and Beauty of the Artificial* continued to evolve.

I found the one existing copy of this work in Harding's books and papers after he died. The text is typed on thin paper and held in thick grey cloth-bound covers. I believe he finished it about 1939, which means it had been a part of his life for seven years. A very important part of his life. Within the circle of his family this book was known as 'Mabel', a rough acronym of the title. The joke was that 'she' was his mistress, which in one sense was right on target since Harding's writing was in some ways more important to him than anything else in his life.

In 1945, at the end of the War, Harding (now Major Harding) returned to England, by which time he was deep into work on *The Hierarchy of Heaven and Earth*. Some important ideas in *The Hierarchy* were first developed in *Mabel,* so in a sense this earlier book was the ground from which that very great book *The Hierarchy* sprang. But *The Hierarchy* so outran *Mabel,* developing Harding's view of the cosmos to such a new and higher level, that *Mabel* became redundant—much like some tools described in *Mabel* were superseded by more evolved ones. And so, valued but now obsolete, it was carefully stored away and probably never seen by anyone, never mind read, till I found it.

From one point of view this book is a window into the character of the young Harding. It is evidence of his energy, determination, ambition and self-confidence. From another point of view it is important as a record of how Harding began working out his brilliant contribution to the way humanity sees itself—his 'new diagram of man in the universe'. But *The Meaning and Beauty of the Artificial* is also worth reading for itself. Celebrating the healing truth that there is no absolute boundary between the self and the world, Harding picks you up on the first page and carries you with his infectious enthusiasm all the way to the final sentence.

Richard Lang

PREFACE

I suppose that my first duty to the prospective reader is to tell him in as few words as possible what he is in for. I do not wish to trick him with a title which a friend of mine, much to my surprise, tells me is a catch-penny phrase, if not a contradiction in terms. For I had quite forgotten for the moment that *artificial* is in some contexts a term of contumely, spoken of things that should be passed by on the other side, of things not possessing beauty or meaning worth the trouble of looking for. The seeming-paradox creeps in because *nature* and *artifice* are words of more than usual ambiguity. But this is no place for precise definitions.

The modern archaeologist discovers the palimpsests of ancient works by taking photographs from the air, so finding at a distance prehistoric evidences where at close quarters he found only wheat-stalks. It is such a view that I wish to present. Both the specialist and the man-in-the-street know a great deal about the material works of man, how they are made and used, and for what reasons they exist. Everyone is interested in new inventions, new buildings, new machines. But these things are so familiar and near to us that we find it difficult to focus our sight clearly upon them. To see them in a clearer perspective we must do mentally what the archaeologist does physically, retire to a distance where bewildering detail merges into broad outlines, if we would grasp the significance of the artificial. It is my purpose, then, to survey from one or two angles the wide territory of man's material achievement. Obviously we shall have no place for technical detail, nor is it my intention to trace the general history of fabrication so much as to correlate this part of man's life with his work in other fields, especially that of biological science. For I believe that all who make and use manufactured things—who does neither?—ought occasionally to see their work as a product and function of life, not only of human life, but of Life as a whole. On the other hand those whose business is to study living forms are not always sufficiently aware that, with lifeless stuff, Life through man is creating new and most wonderful forms which, crude though they are compared with the living, may yet be capable of throwing a side-light upon the Nature to which, after all, they ultimately belong. Polixines tells Perdita, in *The Winter's Tale,* of an 'art which does mend nature—change it rather; but *the art itself is nature.*' To realise this fact more clearly would help those who deal with the 'artificial' and students of 'nature' to a broader understanding of their own and each other's problems. If I succeed in persuading the reader of the value of such a mutual widening of views, half my intention will be fulfilled. The other half is that those of us who are not specialists in either field might see the world of artifice as it were through a diminishing glass, by which the matter of a hundred branches of technical science is condensed into so small a space that we are able to see the broad pattern, which may help to explain the present and suggest the outline of what may follow.

I need hardly remind the reader of the importance of our subject. It is literally a life-and-death matter. Human destiny hangs upon what we shall do with these devices of ours, the machines, now with us for good or ill. How we deal with the problems of industrialism may turn upon our appreciation of the rôle of the artificial no less than upon our answers to the many questions of economics, politics and psychology which are involved.

It has been assumed that the reader has no specialized knowledge of any of the subjects which come under discussion, so that the entire argument shall be as clear as possible to anyone of moderate education. Many, perhaps most of my readers, will therefore find it necessary to skip lightly over those sections which are designed to prepare the ground for the less well-informed. And I must crave indulgence for the way in which many complex problems are summarily disposed of. In so small a book dealing with so large a subject, it is impossible to thrash out thoroughly every question that arises. Where authorities disagree upon major points, however, I have endeavoured either to avoid taking sides, or when that is impossible, to mention the opposing view and to leave the reader to take his choice.

One point I must stress to avoid misunderstanding. We are concerned here with only facts and theories relating to facts, not with moral judgments. Whether this or that actual tendency is for our ultimate good or makes for moral and spiritual loss; whether machines and artefacts of all kinds are, as some say, deplorable engines of mischief, or the destined saviours of the race; whether industrialism leads heaven-wards or hell-wards, and all similar questions, are beyond the scope of this treatise.

The large number of books that I have consulted cannot be listed here: many of them will be found in the foot-notes. Where my work is original, and where derivative, I have tried to make evident. It has consisted largely of building up known facts into a system that is in some parts my own but owes an incalculable debt to writers upon all manner of subjects.

Contents

Adaptation. Variations and mutations. Integration. Natural selection. Sexual selection. Other theories.

The evolution of artificial instruments. Adaptation. Variations and mutations. Integration. Selection.

The general tendencies of evolution among artefacts. Increase of complexity and automatism. Degeneration. Skeuomorphs and vestigial parts. Divergence and convergence. Linear evolution.

Perdita: Sir, the year growing ancient, —
Not yet on summer's death, nor on the birth
Of trembling winter, — the fairest flowers o'the season
Are our carnations, and streak'd gillyvors,
Which some call nature's bastards: of that kind
Our rustic garden's barren; and I care not
To get slips of them.

Polixenes: Wherefore, gentle maiden
Do you neglect them?

Per: For I have heard it said
There is an art which, in their piedness, shares
With great creating nature.

Pol: Say there be;
Yet nature is made better by no mean,
But nature makes that mean; so, o'er that art
Which you say adds to nature, is an art
That nature makes. You see, sweet maid, we marry
A gentler scion to the wildest stock,
And make conceive a bark of baser kind
By bud of nobler race. This is an art
Which does mend nature, — change it rather; but
The art itself is nature.

The Winter's Tale, Act IV, Scene III

CHAPTER I

Nature and Artifice

An inter-stellar traveller would have some difficulty in finding our planet. Its mass is no more than 1/332,000 that of the sun and the sun is but one of perhaps 30,000,000,000 other stars, distributed at fabulous distances from each other in space.

To this relatively infinitesimal speck of matter a strange thing has happened which we cannot be sure has happened anywhere else. A celestial observer of curious temperament, diligent enough to have discovered our existence among the galaxies, might have recorded this event, or rather series of events, somewhat as follows: 'The crust of this Earth has recently acquired the peculiar quality of assuming variable and transient forms. In addition to mountains and valleys, clouds and seas, that are not especially surprising, small green things are to be seen springing mysteriously from the ground and then sinking back again and to become earth once more. These excrescences having covered great areas of the globe, there presently appear among them other portions of this same crust which have become detached and have the power of erratic movement, an attribute they seem to possess in virtue of the substances which flow through them continually. And of late, there has arrived with surprising suddenness a third kind of terrestrial outgrowth, more variable in size and shape and behaviour than the others. Like them it is sometimes able to travel and sometimes it is stationary; like them its individuals are composed of co-ordinated parts, and in some cases so that a stream of matter passes through them and endows them with considerable energy. In short, I find this place extremely odd.'

Such a super-mundane witness of the plant-animal-invention complex to which we belong, would be more than compensated for his ignorance of a great deal that is known to us, by the fact that he would see more of the game than do we who are the players. If we suppose his mind to be like our own, no day-to-day familiarity would have blunted his sense of wonder at what he sees, no practical concern would prevent him from looking at our world disinterestedly, and no 'explanations' would hide from him the fact that next to nothing can be explained. For most of us have never begun to be astonished and all are interested for selfish reasons. The very intelligence with which we try to pry into these things is itself primarily practical and is likely to become more and more biased the nearer it approaches ourselves. But if, by an imaginative effort, we could once get outside ourselves and our business we should be filled with amazement at the never ceasing uprush of rude 'unorganized' matter, which having laid dormant for billions of years, now takes upon itself such splendid forms as the tiger, the delicate flower petal, the bright scales of a butterfly's wing or the subtlest mechanism of the simplest organism, beside which the progress of suns is almost crystal-clear, and eventually appears as those dead but dominant last-comers in a world already full of marvels, huge buildings, swift machines and tentacled cities that engulf or sweep aside all that comes in their way.

We can learn nothing except wonder and humility at such an elevation and must eventually come down to earth and study our subject close at hand. When we come, then, to classify the material objects that make up our environment, we may distinguish three principal sorts: inorganic, vital and artificial things, the last comprising inanimate objects which come of the relations between the others. Accordingly, study of the material world may be divided into three great departments: the first, Physics and Chemistry, which are now practically inseparable, the second, Biology and Sociology, which deal with living organisms, and finally Technical Science, or Technics, as it has been called. The first two groups are sciences of nature, that is to say, of the world as we find it; the third is of art in the widest sense, of the world as men have altered it, are now altering it, and propose to alter it in the future. Suppressing all detail then we have the following scheme:

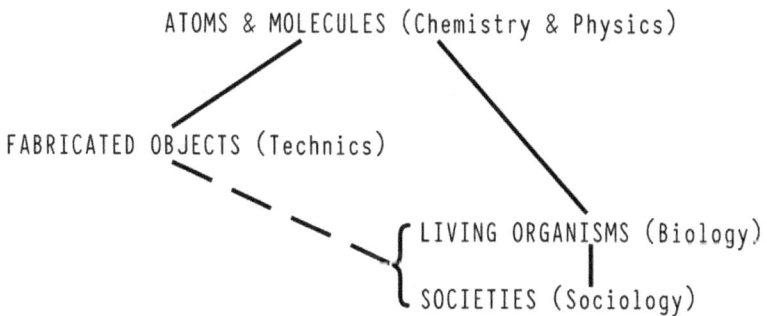

ATOMS & MOLECULES (Chemistry & Physics)

FABRICATED OBJECTS (Technics)

LIVING ORGANISMS (Biology)

SOCIETIES (Sociology)

This diagram is arranged to indicate that the material of the Physicist and the Chemist, consisting of atoms and molecules and so on, is the basis fundamental to the others, which are 'higher' constructions in the scale of things. The dotted line will serve to show the intimate relationship between Technics and the Sciences of Life.

We have, then, provisionally found a place for the Science of the Artificial among its more respectable brethren. What is its present status among them? The fact is that, unlike the others, it has not even the semblance of unity; indeed it can scarcely be said to exist at all. There is no science of artefacts in the sense that there is a science of organisms. There are few who make it their business to investigate the nature of artificial objects with the detachment of the pure scientist, not to use or improve or repeat these objects, but simply to understand them as material phenomena in a world of other material phenomena. And the reason for this neglect is not hard to find. We know so much about the things we have made, else we could never have made them. We can follow their innermost workings. It might be said that here can be nothing to discover; there can be no need for a naturalist of the artificial (if I may use such an expression) to search out the characters of these monsters that share the earth's surface with us. For what a man has invented that at least he understands! Compare our knowledge of the human body with what is known of locomotives and ancient buildings, or our information about the behaviour of protoplasm with the engineer's knowledge of the stresses and strains in the members of his steel bridge, and it will be clear why there are no chairs of the philosophy of the artificial in our universities. Strangely enough, because man's own works are as an open book, few take the trouble to read what is written there, but because the secrets of nature's works are sealed they are always mysterious and fascinating.

Mr. Gerald Heard in his book about clothes[1] says: 'The Life Force is like a juggler; it is always contriving that we shall watch the hand with which the trick is not being done… Evolution is still active, more active indeed than ever before, but at a different range, on an original circuit… Evolution is going on no longer in but around man, and the faster because working in a less resistant medium.' Can it be that, after all, this stone which the builders of our knowledge have rejected is the head-stone of the corner? That it should occupy at least a place of importance in the structure is what I hope to show.

But first we must know more precisely what we mean by the term *artificial*. Of all words it is one of the most relative and confusing; its meaning depends always upon the point of view of the speaker. Our only course then is to take each of the several points of view in turn and then to arrive at our own definition.

The most accurate use of the word is to describe all that man has done in the world as distinct from what has been done by other agencies, by nature as we say. Opposed to man's activity, set up as a limit to it, is the world as he finds it. And though he may take much pleasure in making things and in the contemplation of his own and other's work, there is a peculiar satisfaction in the contemplation of what is utterly beyond the narrow sphere of human action. 'A tree,' says Pope, 'is a nobler object than a prince in his coronation robes… Education leads us from the admiration of beauty in natural

---

1   *Narcissus*, p. 9 & p. 18

objects, to the admiration of artificial (or customary) excellence… I don't doubt but that a thorough-bred lady might admire the stars, *because* they twinkle like so many candles at a birth-night.' But however anthropomorphic our vision, nature has a kind of holiness. We reverence what we can neither control nor understand. On the other hand, the things that we have made or changed, just because we are, or should be, their masters, evoke no such respect. Every advance of artifice is a Promethean encroachment upon the domain of the gods. So it has come about that the word *artificial* suggests the profane, the false, even the wicked. It seems to imply that man is nature's naughty child, upsetting everywhere an august and orderly household. When he obtrudes his inventions upon the world, builds a railroad across a plain, drives a highway through the hills or spans a river, many feel that he has violated what is half sacred. He has desecrated the countryside. Gods have been outraged and natural beauty destroyed. Nevertheless much remains. Change the earth as he may, sea, sun, stars and sky are there till the end, and time will heal some of the cruellest scars on the face of nature.

This brings us to the second point of view, from which those modifications of the world that are relatively primitive seem to belong to nature. To us as men all man's work is artificial, but to us as civilized, traditions of long standing and ancient inventions appear truly natural. The soil fresh from the plough, rural scenery with hedgerows, dusty lanes, low farm buildings, and all the profoundly altered country-side often has a charm which not even wild nature can surpass. For all these have been with us from time immemorial;

they are ancient and we of the town have had no finger in their making; they are remote from our present thought and endeavour. They are given, outside the limits of our activity. Urban folk find here the restfulness and beauty of what is beyond their life. Take away the horse-plough and the thatched cottages and put a tractor and concrete houses, and at once you have intruded among rural amenities incongruous artificialities. Replace the village fair and the Punch-and-Judy Show by the cinema, or the peasant costume by the ready-made double-breasted productions of the town, and you have encroached upon what is almost nature to the sophisticated. In short, wherever in town and country, there are occupations well rooted in tradition, or old buildings or tools or materials are still in use, there we have the once artificial become, to those who observe but do not participate, parts of nature itself. And perhaps the tractor and the concrete houses, after they have become long out of date and survive only as vestiges of an older civilization, will afford a welcome relief to a man who wishes to escape from an 'over-civilized' community.

Whatever may be alleged against modern civilization, it must be said in extenuation that the pleasure which we derive from the ancient, from the primitive and from raw nature, is enhanced by the contrast afforded by contemporary life. By virtue of this contrast objects and customs which seem ordinary or tiresome, and in any case somewhat artificial, to the habitué wear a beauty for us because we are not involved. It is the feeling of apartness which enables us to enjoy the unfamiliar. There are no practical complications. The farm-house is to the farmer damp or dry, cold or warm in winter, spacious or confined; it has the immediacy of the artificial; to the casual visitor it may appear to be of a piece with the hills and hedges and trees around it. The fields, which are to their owner plots of earth of just such a quality, requiring so much labour and yielding so many bushels to the acre, may seem to the city dweller as remote and unspoiled as the clouds above them.

All the inventions of man must either fall into desuetude or eventually be assimilated by nature in this way. But even the most revolutionary of mechanical devices must obey at every turn natural laws. Man builds machines to change the world only by utilizing more and more thoroughly the laws of the world he alters. He turns nature back upon itself. So it is that every utilitarian production of his is shot through with the same 'nature' as a flower or a snow crystal. Its beauty too is of the same order as theirs; it is a natural beauty, the work of no conscious artist. We have come to our third view-point. All human inventions which are not the result of his 'free' creative imagination, but whose form, down to the last rivet and brick, is dictated by necessity have an appearance of a naturalness to the man who looks at the world with an artist's eye. Only to a few do the aeroplane, the dynamo and the grain silo have a beauty that is refreshing because it is unconscious. Those who create what is free from the restraint of usefulness may find in such things the inspiration of a beauty that is given, that is free from all aesthetic intention, that is rooted and grounded in the nature of things. To most people the machine is the very essence and symbol of artificiality. But to some few it has the undeliberate 'rightness' of the organism; every part of the aeroplane is as sufficient and unquestionable as a bird's wing and feathers; the sleek economy of the precisely organized is nowhere spoiled by artificial extravagances. Just as from our first view-point, the plough and the spade spoil the spontaneity of the virgin country, and from our second, the railway line and the factory offend among lanes and meadows, so from this third position, the decoration of the strictly utilitarian with free ornament is alike deplorable. It is artificial. It is human trespass in a natural world where only the useless is vile. But if this embellishment should chance to follow the necessary form, there will be as little blame as when a man puts a rustic fence around his garden. When, however, the four orders of classic architecture are applied to the façade of a sausage factory, or a fresco of water lilies to the interior of a fast automobile,—this is a preposterous meddling with nature, in a word, gross artificiality.

So within our category of the artificial there remains now only art, for material purposes the least useful of all human activities, and, in a sense, the most artificial. But, though he is under no necessity to write poems which are historically true, nor to paint or to sculpt what he sees around him, the mind of the artist belongs to the life stream; his works are the works of life. He is an instrument only. The most extravagant or sublime flight of his imagination cannot depart a hair's breadth from the nature which includes himself. In fact we find that what might be called, in Perdita's words, 'nature's bastards' are all her most legitimate children. Intellect must bend to an external nature; instinct is the expression of an internal nature. Search below the surface and the artificial slips through your fingers. It is a mere shadow of the mind which divides the world into the 'I' and the 'not-I', a product of the inevitable duality of thought.

Only our first use of the word artificial remains more or less constant for every man, that is, to distinguish all men's artefacts from nature's raw material. This use, therefore, we will adopt, always realizing as we do so that below artifice lies nature. Strive against her as you may, you will only obey her as faithfully as her most subservient minion.

CHAPTER II

The Instruments of the Animal

An artifact is essentially an instrument of life, a tool, an aid to living. Our principal concern is with the instruments of man, but when we come to search for the origins of his faculty of making and using tools, we are taken back to the crude implements of early cultures, and further to cruder instruments of mammals, and beyond even these to the works of the most primitive of organisms. For what can a bird's nest, a spider's web or a worm's hole in the ground be but instruments of their life, environment turned to good use, and has not even the most minute of creatures done something to change its world? We are bound, accordingly, to turn for information to the stock whence we came, to find those tendencies working darkly there which culminate in our own life.

But first let us take a glance at this remarkable parcel of matter which we call an organism. It is composed of precisely the same kinds of atoms as those that are to be found in the earth and air of which it is part. But in the body of the organism these basic materials are arranged in highly complex patterns, so complex that we have only begun to unravel them. It is an elaborate mechanism, emerging at a higher level than its constituent atoms and molecules, ceaselessly active and always exchanging energy with its environment. As Spencer puts it, life is 'the continuous adjustment of internal relations to external relations.' For five days or five hundred years the organism may keep up its expenditure of energy and replace what it uses. This energy is obtained by the combustion of the food which has been built up into the material of its body, somewhat as the candle releases heat and light when its tallow is oxidized. But unlike the candle, the living creature absorbs new materials to replace what has been broken down, and builds them up into complex unstable compounds which are again oxidized with the release of more energy. An organism may thus be looked upon as a laboratory for the transformation of energy, that is used to maintain equilibrium with its environment. What is left over after 'establishment charges' have been met is available for growth and reproduction.

Every organism consists of cells, sometimes of many millions, though most commence life as a single cell and a large number never get beyond this stage. This living unit of all plants and animals is a minute mass of colloidal substance called protoplasm, and is capable of assimilating food and growing, of responding to certain stimuli, and usually of reproduction by dividing into two parts when it has reached a certain size. Where these two 'daughter cells' remain together, continue to multiply, and eventually produce cells which are differentiated into particular kinds, of which each variety has its special structure and function, (as, for instance, nerve cells, muscle cells, blood corpuscles, etc.) we have a multicellular organism with its complement of organs. But where, after division, daughter cells part, lead a separate existence, and remain similar in structure, we have the unicellular plants and animals known as Protista. And all

Chapter II—The Instruments of the Animal

known living things, plant or animal, single-celled or many-celled, have arisen in this way from other cells. Never has inanimate matter been seen to generate the living.

The Amoeba is a convenient example to take. This microscopic animal consists of a single cell containing protoplasm within a thin enveloping wall. Its shape changes continually as it moves about at the bottom of the pond, throwing out irregular projections of its body and retracting them again. It has no permanent limbs, for its whole body is a locomotory organ. Through the microscope one can see that its protoplasm is not homogeneous. A rounded body called the nucleus, consisting of a different kind of protoplasm from the rest, occupies almost any position within the cell. Darker bodies surrounded by clear liquid are food particles in the process of digestion. Its food the Amoeba has discovered during its wanderings, distinguished it from inedible material—exactly how, remains a mystery,—and enveloped it by projecting the necessary pseudopodia, or temporary limbs. Another body lodged in the protoplasm near to the surface of the cell is the contractile vacuole, which gradually grows larger and then suddenly disappears, ejecting its contents into the surrounding water.

Perhaps the appearance of the Amoeba is not startling. But consider its behaviour. This minute body performs all the essential functions of the animal. It moves about, recognizes its food, digests it, eliminates the waste, builds the rest up into protoplasm and grows; it breathes by absorbing oxygen from the water; and most wonderful of all, after it has reached a certain size, profound changes take place within it: the nucleus behaves in a very strange fashion and eventually is divided into two, a medial constriction of the cell body appears, and the original cell has become two independent daughter cells. The structure and behaviour, during cell division and ordinary life, of both the nucleus and the surrounding protoplasm are exceedingly complex. Much is known but this is insignificant beside what remains to be discovered. And the Amoeba belongs to the least intricate class of organisms.

We are looking for the first evidences of tools. We might have expected to discover at this low level of life only the most rudimentary of instruments. But instead, what do we find? A creature that is itself an infinitely subtle system of instruments. A kit of tools that are in their own way perfect, and an instinctive but none the less skilful operator. As Bergson says, after having described the tools of men, 'Does an unintelligent animal also possess tools or machines? Yes, certainly, but here the instrument also forms part of the body that uses it; and, corresponding to this instrument, there is an *instinct* that knows how to use it.' [1] It is true the Amoeba has no artificial tools. Because its natural ones are so adequate and its needs so restricted, such aids and props of life are quite unnecessary. And not only have nature's instruments a subtlety far surpassing the most delicate of artefacts, but they have an adaptability in use that the artificial can rarely imitate, and they operate upon entirely different principles: the chemical changes in the material of the living machine itself provide its energy for action, and above all, the organism appears to be capable of learning by experience.

---

[1]   *Evolution Creatrice*, English Translation, p. 146

But if the Amoeba is thus efficiently equipped, so are other organisms and ourselves also. With our emphasis upon intelligence, we are inclined to forget that we have a knowledge of a deeper unconscious kind that is able to control perfectly the undeliberate functions of the body, and that a mere hair of the head is a more delicate and wonderful structure than all the workshops of the world could contrive. In a manner of speaking, the stupidest village idiot performs instinctively actions that all the savants cannot explain, far less imitate artificially. Because of the manifest advantages of intellect we are often tricked into forgetting that, as an iceberg has a mere fraction of its bulk above the water, so our unconscious 'knowledge' penetrates the depths of life, leaving above the level of consciousness only the superficial structure of intelligence.

But this, you may say, is not the kind of tool with which we are concerned. Nevertheless, though the bodily tool is radically different from the artificial, the laws of their development are in some ways similar; there is a family likeness between them, and both exist for the same purpose. And that purpose is a dual one: to adapt the organism to its environment, and to actively change this environment into a place in which the organism is likely to flourish.

These two aspects of the organism, passive and active respectively, provide a useful interpretation of the use of all instruments, whether natural or artificial. In some degree every living creature is modified by its environment and, in return, modifies its environment. Life is best understood as this reciprocating activity. Whether an organism inclines more towards the inactive or towards the aggressive side, is moulded by circumstances or moulds them, is not determined by the efficiency of its instruments. For efficient they must be, else the organism perishes. Every organism is thoroughly adapted to its circumstances. Adaptation means nothing more nor less than the perfecting of instruments, and it may proceed in two ways, by the perfecting of the bodily instrument, or by the perfecting of the external instrument, that is, by improving the environment. As Professor Whitehead points out, 'There are two sides to the machinery involved in the development of nature. On the one side, there is a given environment with organisms adapting themselves to it... From this point of view, there is a given amount of material, and only a limited number of organisms can take advantage of it. The givenness of the environment dominates everything... The other side of the evolutionary machinery, the neglected side, is expressed by the word *creativeness*. The organisms can create their own environment.' [2] If the organism makes almost no mark upon the world, if it is unable to change circumstances perceptibly to its advantage, then its own body must be capable of dealing satisfactorily with raw external conditions, taking what influences come its way and either resisting or utilizing them. *Its body thus becomes a set of tools so finely organized that it is capable of using the world as a ready-made instrument, not an artificial one, but a vast natural instrument employed by the species.* The plants, for example, have become such that sun, rain, the oxygen of the air and the salts of the earth are all, without any need for external change, contributory to their existence. But a price must be paid for such

---

2   *Science and The Modern World*, Ch. VI

advantages,—the creature's bodily organization must comply with, be utterly dominated by its environment.

At the next stage there is a certain advance upon this mastery of the organism by its circumstances. The living creature begins, not yet to create its own instruments, but to select nature's more actively. Any environment will not suffice; special local conditions must be found. Clefts in the rock, natural shelters from foe and storm, regions where temperature and water supply are favourable, are discovered and utilized by the more active animal. It selects rather than changes nature, but selection is a step towards full creativeness.

Setting out from such beginnings evolution works outwards. At first organisms are at the mercy of conditions, then they *select* from among given circumstances, and finally, at the highest level, *change* them, *creating a third kind of instrument, interposed between the bodily outfit and the unchanged external instruments.* This new set of tools supplements the body of the organism, adding to it further means of using or resisting forces in the outside world. But as these external instruments are added, and the organism acquires the bodily organization capable of using them to good effect, the greater is its reliance upon these tools and the less able it is to subsist without them. So we may say that evolution has involved an improvement in the efficiency of external instruments and a corresponding decline in the ability of bodily instruments to deal with environment apart from such external aids. While the organism may increase in complexity along with its exterior tools (on the other hand, it may decline) it relinquishes its self-sufficiency, it remains no longer complete in itself. This is clearly to be seen in our own case. We have become thoroughly dependent upon our tools for our livelihood. Remove these: clothing, weapons, fire, shelter and implements, and, at any rate in our climate, all but those who could replace these necessities would perish. But the artefacts of man are the culmination of an evolutionary tendency which we have still to trace.

First let us note that though every living creature changes the world, however slightly, it is only when such modifications definitely improve its environment for it, that we find the beginnings of external creativeness and tools or instruments of our third kind.

The first living things that appeared on the earth must have subsisted upon inorganic matter as most plants do now, for there was no alternative. But later came creatures that preyed upon the plants. To animals the plant is the most indispensable of all tools. So far we have observed only the lifeless external instrument, but here is one that lives, and does so, from the animal's point of view, solely to build up from inorganic matter an abundant food supply. All animals from Amoeba to man have in plants a huge efficient chemical factory capable of turning earth, air and sunshine into the complex organic compounds which alone enable them to exist. We animals are all parasites upon vegetables, directly and indirectly. But this characteristic of ours has not, on the whole, led to bodily degeneration, for to it must be attributed the activeness and mobility of animals which have to search for their food, instead of, like the plants, devouring what comes their way.

Such an onslaught has undoubtedly had its effect upon the plants. If, as seems likely, those species of plants have tended to survive in the struggle for life which were either inedible or had an abundance of edible material, sufficient to supply both their own needs and those of the herbivores, then the herbivores have influenced the course of vegetable evolution to their own advantage. Working slowly and quite unconsciously, animals have helped to make the plants what they are, but man has by a different method carried the process much further. By intelligent control and speedily, he has worked along the same lines as animals before him, and modified the plants upon which he feeds. Not by natural, but by deliberate artificial selection, he has created out of the older plant forms thousands of new varieties and even new species, with many times the food value of the original stocks. For though he is unable as yet to employ purely artificial methods for synthesizing his food, he can improve nature's. Eventually he may imitate them.

Not all animals, however, feed upon plants at first hand. Predators who hunt down and devour other animals get their food in a more concentrated condition,—bulk for bulk, flesh is more nourishing than green-stuff,—but for finding and overcoming their prey, swifter movement, keener smell and sight, and a highly efficient sensory-motor apparatus are needed. Again the use of living instruments, which is really a kind of parasitism, has led to increased activeness and bodily efficiency.

The true parasite has adopted a different attitude to its instrument, or host. Whereas the predator destroys its instruments as it employs them and so is bound to find others to take their pace, the typical parasite settles down to exploit one host, using it as a permanent food-getter. It would clearly be to the parasite's advantage to avoid doing great injury to its instrument, when to obtain another would be difficult or impossible. Accordingly, in the course of evolution, both parasite and host tend to become adapted to one another, so that the harm done by the former tends to decrease as it becomes more adapted to its environment and as its host becomes more or less immune from serious damage. In many ways the parasite changes. It may once have been an active animal with the complement of organs necessary to a roving life, but when, for instance, it makes its home within the stomach or the intestine or the blood stream of an animal and obtains its food through the agency of its host, many of the organs which were valuable in its free condition are now useless encumbrances destined to disappear. Eventually the parasite may lose almost all traces of its former condition. The crustacean *Sacculina*, for example, has descended from ancestors not unlike the crab on which it feeds; now it is a bag, without a vestige of segmentation, without limbs and the muscles and nervous system which operated these, even without an alimentary canal. Every part, except its sexual organs, has degenerated. But there are always some compensations for such losses. Many parasites have developed remarkable characters enabling them to survive in their peculiar environments and to propagate their species under difficult conditions.

The thorough-going parasite, having adopted for life a host, modifies this a little in the course of evolution, but itself is modified a great deal. Though its requirements differ from theirs, the parasite has, like the plants, food ready to hand, provided by an adequate instrument not under its control; like the plants, the parasite is dominated by its environment, having ceased to make shift for itself. The crab gets the living for *Sacculina,* and to do so employs organs and senses similar to those which the parasite has relinquished. Since the latter employs a complex instrument that is completely able to look after itself, some of the parasite's own bodily instruments have become redundant. The analogy which might be drawn between this state of affairs and the condition of a man in a modern society must be left for a later chapter. Here it is sufficient to note the manner in which the external instrument supplements and perhaps eventually 'takes over' entirely, many of the bodily instruments of its user.

But parasitic association between organisms is an extreme instance of the interdependence of lives. More pleasant to contemplate are instances of commensalisms, where the living instrument suffers no harm, though it derives no benefit in exchange for services rendered, and more pleasant still, the symbiotic associations so common in nature, where each party provides something that the other needs. There are, of course, no definite boundary lines between these modes of life; one fades off into the other, and it is often difficult to determine whether an organism shall be called a predator or a parasite, a symbiont or a commensal.

Actually the lives of organisms are interwoven to a degree that is little realized; co-operation exists everywhere and between the most unlikely individuals. We need do no more than take a few examples to indicate the many ways in which living creatures use one another as instruments.

We may commence with a case that reminds us of our own tools. This is the symbiotic partnership between crab *Melia* and a sea-anemone, which is carried about in the crab's claws and used as a weapon and a food-getter. [3] A similar association, this time an instance of commensalism, occurs between a sea-anemone and a species of hermit crab, where the anemone fixes itself to the borrowed whelk shell of the crab and seizes small particles of food as they float by.

The cultivation of plants and the herding and protection of animals that have been domesticated, mark a considerable advance in the control by the organism of its environment. Strangely enough the ants and the termites, millions of years before the dawn of human civilization, had developed the arts of husbandry and stockfarming. W. M. Wheller, the great entomologist, describes the fungus gardens of certain termites thus: 'In section the nests are seen to contain a number of large spherical chambers surrounding the royal cell and connected with it and with one another by galleries. In each chamber there are one or more fungus gardens—sponge-like bodies varying in size from that of a walnut to that of a coconut... They consist of vegetable material which has been collected and comminuted by the workers, passed through their intestines and built up in such a manner as to present a maximum area of surface for the growth of the fungi... According to Bugnion, the mycelium is sown automatically

---

3   Geoffrey Lapage, *Parasites*, p. 9

by the worker termites, since they feed on fungus infected-wood and the conidia pass through their bodies without injury. The fungus gardens are really the nursery of the termitarium and are full of just hatched young, which crop the food-bodies like so many snow-white sheep. Neither the workers nor the soldiers feed on the fungus, but the king and queen and other reproductive forms receive the same food as the young.' [4]

This remarkable association is not so clearly a case of symbiosis as those which Professor Wheeler goes on to describe. The termites have a custom of entertaining a number of guests that we should, in like circumstances, call domestic animals. Of these guests there are several hundred species, some of which however are only tolerated by the termites, while others are definitely parasitic. The true guests are tended and fed by their hosts in return for the bodily secretions they yield, to which the termites are greatly addicted. Many of these guests have become astonishingly adapted to a lazy life in the termitarium: the head has often become smaller and the abdomen and exuderia (the organs of secretion) very large and of monstrous shape. As for the guests of ants, fully two thousand species have been discovered and these include members of nearly all the orders of insects, as well as spiders, mites, millipedes and land crustaceans. Those of them which secrete the fluids beloved of the ants, are really, from the ants' point of view, nothing else than animated sweet factories or breweries, which, supplied with odds and ends, turn these without further trouble into delicious beverages which may be tapped at any

---

4   *Social Life among the Insects*, p. 270

time. Raw material must be provided, but that done, everything else takes care of itself. And so valuable are these living laboratories that when the nest is in danger their hosts have been seen to carry them to safety before attending to their own larvae and pupae. Again we see how, unconsciously, but none the less surely, organisms have helped to make their living tools more serviceable, improved greatly their efficiency and been responsible for the most drastic changes in their structure and behaviour. The mechanism of natural selection has worked so that the ants, over a period of perhaps millions of years, have indirectly created from given material their own instruments, and most adequate instruments these are for their purpose.

These are external food converters. There is another kind of organism, used by the termite for a somewhat similar purpose, that exists within its own body but is not part of it. In the intestines of termites have been found numerous *infusoria* which appear to break down particles of wood into substances that the termite can assimilate. Unfortunately for us, the larva of the Deathwatch beetle is similarly indebted to a yeast plant, situated at the beginning of the digestive part of its food canal. Owing entirely to the good services of this plant the beetle is able to digest the oak rafters of our churches and cathedrals. Buchner discovered that the female, when depositing an egg, releases some yeast plants from two reservoirs associated with her egg-laying apparatus. The plants are eaten by the young larva when it hatches and fulfil their function in its subsequent life. [5] We have here a glimpse of a milder side of nature that would content the

---

5   Op. Cit. P.280, & P. Geddes and J.A. Thomson, *Biology,* p. 93

most scrupulous of moralists, whatever the opinion of the church-warden.

Not having achieved the fabricated tool, which requires a degree of intelligence lacking among the insects, instinct employs living tools in some extraordinary ways. These instruments are used for all sorts of purposes, but for what stranger end than that of a storage vessel, an animated barrel? Yet, among the honey-pot ants, when an abundant supply of honey-dew is available, some of them imbibe so much of this nectar that their abdomens become enormously distended. In such a condition they are quite incapable of walking and are suspended from the ceiling of the nest to await the dry season, when, at the solicitation of the thirsty workers, these living reservoirs regurgitate drops of the precious liquid. Or a living creature may be used by another for protection and concealment. The spider crab that selects a suitable frond of seaweed and painstakingly plants it on its back has donned nothing else than a live suit of clothes, for concealment, not for display. A somewhat more roundabout way of gaining defenders is by imitating protective colours. Thus certain butterflies are distasteful to birds, which, recognizing these insects by their distinctive markings or colours, rarely devour them; but other species of butterflies not necessarily distasteful, have come to resemble very closely those with 'warning colours' and enjoy a similar immunity. Yet another use which an organism may find for other creatures, is that of providing building material. A Javan tree-ant, having no bodily building materials as the spiders have, and being unable to make them from raw material, employs as artisan a caterpillar that provides a silk valuable for binding together the walls of the nest. In return for this service the caterpillar's wages seem considerable,—the young of its employers for food! [6]

But of all co-operative partnerships those between certain insects and flowering plants are the most famous and have led to the most beautiful results. It is necessary for the plant to reproduce itself, and for this purpose the pollen from the anthers must somehow be transferred to the pistil and so to the ovary. Many flowering plants rely upon the wind to do this, but others, by holding out the inducements of nectar and pollen, and advertising these gifts by brilliant colours and subtle scents, prevail upon insects to visit them. While nectar gathering, the guest inadvertently brushes some of the pollen from the male organs onto the female organs of the plants and so ensures their fertility. This intimate association or biocoenose, has led to extreme modifications in both the plants and insects concerned. The insect, for instance, sometimes lives entirely upon the products of the flowers, for obtaining which it has developed a tongue of extraordinary length, while the flower owes its brilliant colours, its peculiar shape, its scent and its nectar to the selection exercised by the insects. Darwin found it to be 'an invariable rule that when a flower is fertilized by wind it never has a gaily coloured corolla.' [7]

We have seen sufficient to realize that organisms cannot be looked upon as entirely independent individuals. For they belong to a vast heterogeneous society, where each affects profoundly many

---

6   *Biology,* Geddes and Thomson, p. 92
7   Quoted by Lubbock, *British Wild Flowers,* p. 8

others and lives are intertwined. Now, as a rule, we do not say that the living tool was *made* by its user, but that each influenced the other's development in the course of evolution. But what do we mean by *made*? When a man makes an implement he alters matter till it corresponds with his preconceived design; he does not create the tool out of nothing. A hatchet, a spear and a club are practically useless forms given a useful shape. As an individual the insect does not make its tools, but in the course of time insects have given their raw material, the flowering plants, a more useful form. It is true that the 'blind' and impersonal machinery of natural selection has been largely, if not entirely, responsible for the changes in both the flowers and their insect visitors, and that it would be mistaken to look for cunning intentions; nevertheless there is here, as we may find so often elsewhere, a foreshadowing of the processes which in man become deliberate and intelligent. For wherever the organism uses living instruments, it must change these, whether consciously or not, and be changed by them. This is the creativeness from which none may escape; it is nothing more nor less than one aspect of the influence of environment upon the organism and of the organism upon its environment. Such creativeness has its roots in the nature of life itself, and the man who shifts and alters his world intelligently, building artificial tools for himself, is at essentially the same business as the insect that changes the shape and colour and scent of flowers, even though the changing may have the appearance of accident, and the time taken may be reckoned in hundreds of thousands and millions of years. It is the slowness with which the lower creatures change their tools which obscures from us the thoroughness of their fabrication. If we could hurry up nature's time-scale and see brought about in a day the changes of a million years, we should see living creatures moulding one another, improving each other's efficiency as instruments of their life, and we should be forcibly reminded of our own operations in the artificial field.

So far we have considered the organism's corporeal tools and the inanimate and living environments which it presses into service. We are approaching the central object of our search—fabrication from inert matter. But there remains one other kind of tool, intermediate between the bodily instrument and the external one, the tool that is made out of the body of the organism that uses it. We make our implements by working upon outside matter. The spider has a different method. By passing raw material through its own body it obtains a perfect manufactured product; it has here an incomparable silk factory capable of turning out a number of different kinds of thread. Its body is a tool to make a tool—the web.

The spider has arrived at the peak of such achievement. Every organism, however, may be regarded as a mechanism through which matter flows continually and undergoes change, and not a few make use of the resultant material. Some beetle larvae, for instance, are said to impregnate the sides of their burrows with urine so that the earth shall harden into resistant concrete. [8] In sexual reproduction we have the manufacture by the male and female of spermatozoa and ova respectively; among birds and reptiles the egg cell is provided with food yolk derived from the female's body, and mammals suckle

8   J.H. Fabre, *Social Life in the Insect World*

their young—these are familiar aspects of the body as a converter of heterogeneous foodstuffs into useful external products. Here we are more concerned with the building of instruments with which the organism supplements those which are already attached to the body. From a host of available examples we may take a few.

Spiders and insects have made the most conspicuous use of bodily products. But some birds also have adopted the same method; the famous bird's nest soup is prepared from the nests of a kind of swift, which are entirely composed of the bird's hardened saliva. Everyone knows, too, how the 'silk-worm' and thousands of other caterpillars spin silken cocoons in which to pass the pupa stage before emerging as perfect insects. These cocoons are often works of considerable beauty and delicateness. Frequently we find what at first sight appears to be forethought of a remarkable kind, as of the caterpillar that securely binds the leaf within which it is about to pass the chrysalis stage, to the main stem of the plant, so that when autumn comes the leaf does not fall to the ground with the rest. Another kind of caterpillar lives gregariously in a silken nest at the top of a pine tree. All descend daily in Indian file to feed upon the pine needles, each leaving behind itself a trail of silk which forms a sort of roadway that will infallibly lead them, Ariadne-wise, back to home and safety after the night's meal. [9]

Silk is a very versatile material, and the spiders in particular have put it to a great variety of uses: for nest building and safety lines, for enveloping their prey in a kind of straight-jacket and for sailing

---

9   J.H. Fabre, *Wonders of Instinct*, p. 125 et seq.

in the air, as well as for the more familiar snaring web. Many web-less spiders trail out behind them wherever they go a thread which serves as a safety line in case of accident. On any sun-bathed wall in the garden the crab-like hunters may be seen creeping, by almost imperceptible movements, towards a resting fly and at last leaping onto it. Should the spider miss its foothold no harm is done for it swings by the thread to which it is attached. Some have attributed the origin of the radiating web to the radiating trails laid in the course of many excursions from a hiding place. However that may be, the fully developed web is exceedingly fine building and has a variability according to conditions that is remarkable at the instinctive level.

The *Epeirae* or garden spiders, for example, construct large and elegant webs. First a triangular or trapezoidal frame is suspended in an approximately vertical plane from the leaves and twigs available, and this serves as a preliminary scaffolding across the web. Over this frame one thread is now drawn, and a small spot of silk near the middle of it marks the centre of the wheel. Then, starting always from the perimeter, the spider lays the radii which converge upon the centre of the web. Though not constructed consecutively, the spokes when completed are very near equidistant and their number is more or less constant for each species. The next portion to be built is the resting place in the centre, which the spider constructs by turning round and round, bridging the radii with a spiral of fine silk. Then follows the construction of an auxiliary spiral at a greater distance from the centre, but this is demolished as the true spiral takes its place. The latter is commenced from the outer edge of the web, the spider deftly fastening the threads emerging from its spinnerets to the spokes of the wheel, by a swift movement of the body. Only this spiral thread is sticky; for all its fineness it is no simple thread, but a pair of twisted hollow tubes containing a glutinous fluid which percolates through to the outside and ensnares the fly. Finally, from the centre of the web to some sanctuary under the leaves is stretched what Fabre calls the telegraph wire. In its retreat the *Epeira* rests motionless and hidden, with one foreleg raised and resting on this communicating thread. If a fly is caught in the web the spider immediately recognizes the vibrations telegraphed and rushes forward, but if the wind shakes the web or one tries to imitate the motions of a victim by disturbing the web with a stick, the spider remains imperturbed.

There are many other varieties of vertical web. Those of the Argiopid spiders, for instance, are even more beautiful accomplishments than *Epeira's;* besides having a more perfect symmetry, four cross patterns radiate from the centre and perhaps serve to divert attention from the spider seated there—the suggestion that these patterns are the result of a desire of the spider's to ornament its web is of course no more than a picturesque fiction. There are, too, webs of a quite different kind, such as those of the *Tegenaria,* which consist of a triangular horizontal sheet of silk, with a maze of threads stretched above it and a tubular lurking place for the spider in the corner. As soon as a victim is trapped in the threads and falls onto the sheet below the spider hurries forward and attacks it.

Many spiders are as skilful at nest building as others are at snare building. *Argyroneta,* the water spider, spins a most remarkable home and nursery in the shape of a diving bell, which is supplied with air brought down in bubbles by the spider. The *Epeira's* nest is also worthy of notice; it is a silken bag with a delicately scalloped rim, suspended by threads in a convenient place. The innermost portion of the nest contains the eggs resting in a very fine silken pocket, around which is a packing of brown silk, and the whole is enveloped in a stronger waterproof casing of white, brown and black threads—a nest worthy of a versatile weaver of the geometrical web.

The only other secreted building material that will compare in importance with silk is the wax of the bees. This substance is produced by glands situated between the abdominal segments of the insect and is used to build the hexagonal cells which are to contain the honey, pollen lumps and the larvae and pupae. The *Meliponinae* dilute their wax with earth, resin and other substances, and many other insects use building materials which are partly composed of secretions and partly of extraneous material.

Life has often been described as an experimenter. When she has chanced upon a method of pursuing her ends, it is exploited with successful or disastrous results for the organism. One road may lead to a cul-de-sac, to stagnation or perhaps eventual extinction, another may lead to a swifter Nemesis, but by a third road the organism may progress to higher things. Actually, it is at least doubtful whether we may give such a teleological interpretation to nature, but when describing the procedure of evolution it is very difficult to avoid doing so. Here we may postpone the question by saying that it is *as though* Life has a purpose in view of which she is dimly aware. We may say, then, that Life, in her search for instruments to increase the creativeness of the individual, appears to have explored in various directions. Her first essays were with a set of bodily instruments dominated by raw, unmitigated environment; then another living creature was used as tool, as medium for exploiting the world. The third road, the use of bodily secretions to make instruments, we have just examined. Here we have *fabrication,* not yet intelligent, not yet wholly exterior to the fabricator, but nevertheless the construction by the individual of an inanimate tool, extending, as it were, the bodily organs. The advantage of such instruments over those which remain part of the animal's body, is considerable. The spider, with a foreleg resting on the communicating thread of its web, captures its prey by means of a detached portion of its body—yet not detached, for spider and snare are still continuous. The essential difference between bodily and external organs is rather that the organism is committed to the former for life; once this living tool is injured the organism is injured, whereas the dead external tool, though often no less essential, can readily be exchanged for another if it becomes inadequate or is destroyed. *Epeira's* web is no less truly its instrument (or organ) than its eyes or maxilla. In fact, though the spider may survive the amputation of a leg, deprived continually of its webs it will perish. By a method which we call natural, but which from *Epeira's* point of view, if it may be said to have one, is really artificial or creative, this creature has contrived to add to its stature a good deal more than one cubit.

The spider has furnished us with an example intermediate between the corporeal tool and the tool made out of external substances. This last is the fourth kind of instrument discovered by Life, and, if we may judge by results to date, in some respects the most successful of them all. But the device was implicit from the start. The beetle larva that gnaws its way through a tree, builds, or rather excavates, a home as it feeds. It cannot avoid a kind of negative fabrication. The first homes were carved out of the solid and were merely incidental to the business of feeding, but many animals have taken up residence in materials which have not the advantage of providing food as well as shelter. Ants, for instance, tunnel irregular labyrinths of galleries and chambers by removing the earth piece-meal and carrying it away. This is mere building by destruction, but it is an easy step from this to making some use of the material excavated. How this may be done is admirably illustrated by *Odynerus,* a solitary wasp described by Fabre. The insect digs a tunnel in the soil and a chamber at the end of it to receive its egg and a provision of caterpillars. Instead of casting the earth from the hole onto one side, *Odynerus* collects it into small pellets, which are built up round the mouth of the opening and form at last a tube with the orifice turned downwards. But this remarkable structure is merely a temporary convenience, of which the apparent purpose is to provide the wasp with easily accessible material for filling in the hole, after the chamber has been supplied with a sufficient number of caterpillars. Piece by piece the delicate tube is demolished till not a trace of the nest remains. [10]

There are no fewer than ten thousand known species of wasps,

10   *The Mason Wasps,* p. 28 et seq

and of these many construct nests that surpass the incidental work of *Odynerus*. *Eumenes* builds a spherical structure of about an inch in diameter, with an opening at the top like the mouth of a jar. The insect compounds a mortar of dust and saliva which it builds up ring by ring, diminishing and increasing with admirable accuracy. From time to time it selects small stones, carries them to the nest, and pushes them into the yet unhardened mortar, till the whole forms a strong and waterproof jar destined to accommodate the egg and provisions for the larva. Here, as in so many cases, the insect binds together its building materials with bodily secretions. The notorious *Tarantula* spider reinforces the top of its burrow and the parapet with silk, while the *Clotho* is reported to suspend grains of sand from its dish-shaped web in order to prevent the wind from spoiling it. Miss Cheesman discovered in Tahiti a caterpillar whose food consisted of a tree fungus, in which the caterpillar burrows, throwing up around its hole a turret consisting of pieces of fungus held together by strands of silk. But for this defence the caterpillar would immediately be attacked by numerous species of ants. [11]

Another industrious worker with less pleasant but entirely extraneous material is the dung beetle. It devours this second-hand food in great quantities, but first the beetle builds up a sphere of manure which it trundles along to some retreat where it can take its meal in safety. The female *Scarabaeus* constructs pellets of sheep's dung, in each of which an egg is laid, and buries them. Another species digs a hole no less than five feet deep, at the top of which the

---

[11]   Evelyn Cheesman, *Insect Behaviour*, p. 72

male makes dung pellets and lowers them to the female at the bottom, who tears them up again to provision her eggs. Not less interesting is the behaviour of the Ambrosia beetle, which uses the excrement of its larvae for the cultivation of fungus gardens. [12]

We have noticed the concrete domes of the wasp *Eumenes*. *Pelopaeus*, another wasp, builds in the chimney corner a less durable nest of mud alone, unmixed with saliva. Another material, paper made from wood fibre cemented with some oral secretion, is a favourite among the social wasps, and small pieces of leaves and moss are sometimes used. The Stenogastrine wasps build beautiful hanging nests of decayed wood or earth, long intertwining cylinders of cells, or graceful pear-shaped structures entered from beneath. Many solitary bees also have interesting nests, of which the bumble-bee's is one of the most curious. It is woven of pieces of grass and moss placed in a hole. The female lays her eggs upon a lump of pollen paste in the centre, spreads over them a coating of wax, and sits on them, never leaving the nest until the eggs are hatched. But before laying, she provides herself with a waxen pot containing the honey which will provision her till she is able to leave the nest again. The larger nests of the social bees, with their great numbers of hexagonal cells, are more familiar and in some ways more remarkable even than those of solitary insects. We have seen sufficient, however, of the craftsmanship of instinct to make further illustration unnecessary.

Among the spiders and insects instinct has reached a peak of efficiency. The most distinctive feature of this mode of behaviour, according to the late Dr. Rivers, is that instinct is innate, whereas

12   W.M. Wheeler, Op.Cit., p. 36

intelligence is always acquired. In so far as an organism's behaviour is the result of experience it is intelligent, and in so far as its behaviour is quite independent of experience it is instinctive. Thus without a model to learn from and without any instruction, every action normally necessary to its survival is performed by the insect novice. The newly hatched spider will climb as high as it can, let float its gossamer thread, allow the wind to take it far afield; then it will build a perfectly adequate web by means of which it catches its victims in the manner of its species. There are no clumsy first attempts, no link is missing in the chain of responses to the appropriate stimuli. The spider has inherited, not acquired, its gifts of aeronautics, nest building and snaring. But compared with intelligence, instinct has a rigidity, a lack of adaptability to unfamiliar circumstances, which mars its efficiency. Faced with unusual conditions or interrupted in the course of its routine, instinct often fails. Nevertheless, instinctive behaviour is not altogether inelastic; frequently it is capable of adjustments, which, according to Dr. Rivers, can only be explained by qualities of the same order as those belonging to intelligence. [13]

Among birds and mammals we find an improvement in this capacity to learn by experience, behaviour which begins to show the dim beginnings of reason. At first there is little indication of the

13   See *Instinct and Intelligence*, in Brit. Journ. Psych., Vol III (1910). As an illustration of the breakdown of instinct where fronted with strange conditions, I may mention an experiment which I performed with an Epeira. The spider was placed upon a hoop of suitable size supported above a bowl of water, so that it would not be able to build its web anywhere but inside the hoop. On repeated occasions it failed to do so successfully, only a formless maze of threads resulted. Other spiders of the same species as the first failed also, the reason being, I suppose, that such conditions are not met with in nature, where the spider is used to non-continuous and irregular supports for its web.

new potentialities, and the tools of the vertebrates show little or no advance upon those of the arthropods until man appears. Though the nests of birds do not surpass the work of the mason wasps or the social bees, they are often remarkable when we take into account the paucity of the bodily tools at the bird's disposal. We all know the fine workmanship of the hedgerow bowls, constructed of grass stems lined and interwoven with horsehair and disguised on the outside with leaves and lichen, and the mud nests of the swallow are no less familiar. Exotic birds are sometimes more enterprising. The Hammerhead, for example, builds an enormous structure of mud and sticks, sometimes six feet wide and capable of bearing the weight of a man. The Hornbill, having laid its eggs in a hollow tree, blocks up the opening until only a small hole remains, sufficient to enable the male to pass food through to the hen on the nest. And the hanging nest of the weaver bird, made of long grass stems woven into a rope which hollows out below into the nest chamber, reminds one, though in external appearance only, of the far more delicate work of the paper wasps.

The homes of mammals are poor compared with birds' nests and poorer still compared with the nests of insects. The harvest-mouse uses wheat stalks as columns, weaving its nest of grass around them, and many other rodents contrive some sort of shelter for their young. But of all mammals the beavers are the best famed of builders. A large number of them live gregariously in burrows or lodges near the banks of a stream. To obtain wood for building and for food, they gnaw round the bases of trees till they fall and then float the logs downstream to their lodges. When the timber by the stream has become exhausted, the beavers construct canals and dams to make further supplies available, and in this way large areas of forest are eventually deprived of timber and covered with water. The behaviour of the beaver can only be accounted for by allowing it a degree of intelligence that is almost unrivalled except by man.

Anthropologists have often characterized man as the tool-using animal. The appropriateness of this definition depends upon the meaning we attach to the word *tool,* for there are several kinds or orders of tools. So far we have chiefly considered two of these orders: first the bodily tool, then the tool which comes between the organism and its world, in reality a specially favourable portion of that world. Now we have come to tools of the third order, to those which are of no direct use, mere means to an end. These are tools to make tools. All animals and plants have bodily instruments; very many have tools of the second order. But few, very few indeed, have tools of the third order,—external tools to make tools, and only man has them to a notable degree.

Man is pre-eminently a maker of tools to make tools, but he shares this distinction with a few others, which, like him, have been able to put instruments to uses that are of indirect advantage only. Yet this third mode has been implied, to some degree, in our second. The bird finding a stick for its nest, the mason wasp choosing a stone of the requisite size for its cupula, have with some dim foresight or unwittingly, anticipated the requirements of what they are making and have selected, if they have not made, tools to make tools. Still, the stick and the stone are scarcely tools in themselves but rather parts of an instrument,—the nest. But when we come to the nest building of a certain species of *Sphex* wasp, we find what is in some respects the most advanced behaviour known among insects. After filling in its burrow, which contains the egg and provisions for the larva, *Sphex* searches for a small pebble, which is held between the mandibles and repeatedly used to tamp down the soil over the excavation. This remarkable and isolated case of the selection and use of a temporary tool in the making of another is well authenticated, having been observed by no less than nine entomologists. [14]

It is not until we arrive at the primates—if we except a few tentative essays—that such a performance again occurs. Köhler has observed a monkey fit two sticks together to make a longer one with which to reach a banana lying outside its cage, and pile boxes upon one another in order to reach fruit suspended from the ceiling,—actions which leave no doubt as to the presence of considerable intelligence. [15] An entertaining account of an ape is quoted by Tylor: 'The anthropoid ape Majuka, kept lately in the Zoological Gardens at Dresden, saw how the door of the cage was unlocked, and not only did it herself, but even stole the key and hid it under her arm for future use; after watching the carpenter she seized his bradawl and bored holes with it through the little table she had her meals on; at her meals she not only filled her own cup from a jug, but, what is more remarkable, she carefully stopped pouring before it ran over; when her friend the director of the gardens came to her, she put her arms round his neck,

14   W.M. Wheeler, op. Cit., p. 54
15   *The Mentality of Apes.*

kissed him three times, and then lay down on her bed and giving him her hand fell into her last sleep.' [16] This animal was evidently as clever at using human tools as the one previously described was at constructing its own. Apart, however, from the contact with humans and imitation of them, though wild apes have been seen to use objects as tools, they have never been known to make a tool to hold in the hand. This only man has done, with what consequences we shall see in the next chapter.

---

[16]   E. B. Tylor, *Anthropology,* p. 51. (1913 Ed.)

Weapon shapely, naked, wan,

Head from the mother's bowels drawn,

Wooded flesh and metal bone, limb only one and lip only one,

Grey-blue leaf by red-heat grown, helve produced from a little seed sown,

Resting the grass amid and upon,

To be lean'd and to lean on.

Walt Whitman, Song of the Broad-Axe

CHAPTER III

The Instruments of Man

We have come at last to ourselves, to our creativeness. If we had entertained any idea of our uniqueness in the field of artifice, we must own that we were mistaken. We must recognize that here at least we are homologous with the rest of the animal kingdom, and even with plants, differing from them in degree rather than kind. There is a tendency, which on the whole increases as we rise in the scale of life, for the organism to create around itself a field of influence, a purlieu, a peculiarly favourable sphere which is somehow specialized in the organism's service. With our incurable self-occupation, we call this activity natural when the lower creature performs it, but artificial when we are the actors. Such a distinction has, or should have, no place in science. If the bird's nest is natural then the steam engine is natural also; if the one is artificial then the other is artificial also. For both are creations of the organism, useful instruments interposed between the neutral or unfriendly world and the permanent life-structure of the body.

The history of the animal is necessarily the history of its tools. Both the organism's body and its exterior tools are changed in the course of time and there is a general tendency, though with innumerable exceptions, for the one or the other or both to gain in complexity. Life's aim is apparently to produce ever more efficient instruments, and whatever their character, whether internal or external, dead or alive, its methods are similar in either case. By the evolution of the organism, that is, of its bodily instruments, and by the evolution of the organism's specialized field, that is, of its external instruments, living forms have tended to increase in independence and power over the world. And always the one kind of instrument affects the development of the other. So that when we are considering the evolution of a line of organisms, we are bound to take into account the evolution of all their means of wresting a living from their environment. To attempt to explain the structure of a flowering plant without reference to its insect visitors would clearly be of little use, and the morphology of the bee cannot rightly be interpreted without consulting its instruments, the flowers. The thorough-going parasite shows us how important the instrument may be to its user. The liver fluke gets its living by means of the sheep's body no less than by its own. The spider is scarcely less dependent upon its web. And we would fare badly if we were removed from our social structure with all its tools. While taking care, then, not to overlook their essential differences, we must recognize that bodily and external instruments have an identical function, to maintain the life and resist the destruction of the individual and species to which they belong. *And, in virtue of this common use, these two kinds of instruments of the individual have evolved along similar lines and by similar methods.* There are, as we shall see, most important resemblances (and of course no less important differences) between the ancestral history, or phylogeny, of the living organism and the phylogeny, if we may extend the use of the tem, of the dead artefact. And these are no chance resemblances, no fortuitous analogies, for the same force which is instinct in the primeval protoplasm has worked outwards and caught up in its toils inert matter to supplement the living. What is the artificial but matter which bears the impress, however faint, of life itself? Though the vital forces work intensely within the living tool and but vaguely upon the dead tool from without, both tools are wielded to the same end, both are parts of one complex of weapons in one battle for life.

To make clearer these relationships let us review briefly some of the factors which have gone to make our corporeal tools what they are, and then consider more fully the evolution of the artificial appendages which men have added to these.

The theory of organic evolution has undergone many modifications, from the views of Erasmus Darwin and Lamark to De Vries, and it is still a battleground of biologists. There is, however, a general agreement upon many points, though some authorities stress one factor, and some stress another, as playing a major part in the development of species.

One of the most apparent characteristics of vital organization and function, that any casual observation of nature will reveal, is the universal adaptation of living things to environment. We often speak of this adaptation as desirable for the welfare of the organism, but it is absolutely obligatory. All living species are suited to the conditions under which they live, otherwise their life would immediately cease.

In innumerable ways animals and plants have become modified so as to exploit as many corners of the earth, air and sea, and to gain advantages from each other. If in one respect the adaptation of a species does not seem to have proceeded very far, in another way there will appear the corresponding compensations. Thus, for example, the tortoise and the penguin are poor runners, but the former has an invulnerable suit of mail as a protection from its enemies, and so has no need to run away from them, and the latter has almost altogether avoided the predator by living on barren islands.

Adaptation is to be seen everywhere. We may select a few examples at random, to indicate its thoroughness, from the 'protective resemblances' of insects and other animals. The 'stick' caterpillars not only resemble in shape and colour the twigs of the plants upon which they feed, they have also an instinct which leads them to attach themselves to the stem, remaining inert and stiff, imitating perfectly the appearance of the surrounding twigs and so escaping their enemies. The leaf butterflies have the colour and shape of leaves, possess similar Markings, and rest upon the stem of a plant in the appropriate position, where they are almost impossible to detect. It is well known that arctic animals change their summer colours to white to avoid being seen in the snow. The eggs of many birds are exceedingly difficult to distinguish from the stones among which they are laid. And the flounder resting on the sea bed escapes the most vigilant eye. These are adaptations to a living hostile environment. We might have taken the history of the horse to show how four of its five toes have gradually been reduced in size till they have almost disappeared, leaving one greatly enlarged toe which is an adaptation to life on the grass-lands. But to multiply instances from nature's inexhaustible number of adaptations is unnecessary.

One result of progressive adaptation we may notice in passing. The conditions under which animals live, often lead to unrelated and very differently organized forms assuming a similar external appearance. This tendency is well illustrated by the whales, porpoises and their relations, which, though mammals, have come to resemble fish in many ways, and by bats, also, mammals, whose wings remind us of the wings of birds. Here, of course, the resemblances are in the main superficial, but they go to show that like environments often lead to what is known as convergent evolution. But the pressing question is, how have all these adaptations arisen?

It is plainly a rule that offspring resembles parent. Even the most insignificant characters may be handed down to the next generation. But it is also true that no member of a species exactly resembles any other member. Always there is some slight difference, and sometimes there is a considerable departure from the mean, that is a variation. The male and female germ cells, carrying somewhat different hereditary characters, unite in the fertilized egg, and so arise all manner of combinations. The theory of Mendel and the law of heredity need not detain us here. It will be sufficient to note that variations do occur and that these may be hereditable. The variability of certain plants is common knowledge. Not only is no tree or leaf of precisely the same shape as another, but more important variations in the number of leaflets in a compound leaf, or of petals in a coralla sometimes occur. Again, for example, the contour of a man's head, the pattern and colour of a butterfly's markings, of the configuration of a whelk shell may show considerable fluctuation from type.

Where a more definite break from the normal occurs, entirely new characters appearing which cannot readily be traced in the parents, the new form is called a mutation. Nearly all such deviations are hereditable. T. H. Huxley gives an example of a lamb, born of normal parents, which had a long body and short legs, and so was unable to jump over fences. From this individual a new breed was obtained which preserved this most desirable peculiarity. De Vries, who discovered plants of the evening primrose giving rise to several new forms, believes that new species have arisen in this way rather than by the selection of variations.

Another most important factor in organic evolution is integration, the co-operation of individuals to form another individual of a higher order. The lowest known living things are single cells living separate lives. At the next stage, a number of cells have formed a colony, remaining in physical contiguity without much mutual aid. But where division of labour has set in among the members of such an association, then a new and higher whole has come into being, an individual of a second order. Again, individuals belonging to this second order may enter into intimate and permanent relationships with one another and begin to constitute together a whole of a third order, as some have called a human or insect society. [1]

In these ways then, by variation, mutation, and integration, new material has been constantly provided for nature's sieve. By natural

1   Integration is more fully discussed in Chapter V.

selection those characters which have no value in the struggle tend to be thrown aside, and those which tend to assist the organism are preserved and propagated. There is always a tendency, as Malthus pointed out, for organisms to multiply far beyond the limit required to maintain the numbers of their respective species at a constant level. This inevitably leads to a scramble for the means of livelihood in which varieties possessing favourable attributes will most likely survive. And so have diverged from primitive common ancestors all the hosts of living things, adapted to all sorts of circumstances. In Darwin's own words: 'How do those groups of species, which constitute what are called distinct genera, and which differ from each other more than do the species of the same genus, arise? All these results... follow from the struggle for life. Owing to this struggle, variations, however slight and from whatever cause proceeding, if they be in any degree profitable to the individuals of a species, in their infinitely complex relations to other organic beings and to their physical conditions of life, will tend to the preservation of such individuals, and will generally be inherited by the offspring. The offspring, also, will thus have a better chance of surviving, for, of the many individuals of any species which are periodically born only a small number can survive. I have called this principle, by which each slight variation, if useful, is preserved, by the term Natural Selection, in order to mark its relation to man's power of selection.' [2]

Many of Darwin's supporters over-stated the claims of his theory, maintaining that natural selection alone would account for organic

---

[2] *Origin of Species,* 1901 Ed., p. 45

evolution. But Darwin himself disclaims this view when he says that 'natural selection has been the main but not the exclusive means of modification' and admits that disuse of organs may possibly reduce their size eventually. This was the contention of Lamark, who preceded Darwin by a generation. According to the famous Larmarkian theory, bodily modifications acquired during an individual's lifetime, such as an increment in the size of a muscle due to its greater use, or the muscle's diminution due to lack of exercise, as well as direct effects of environment upon the organism, may be inherited and so lead to divergent evolution. This view has been opposed by many scientists, including the great Weissman, who held that no habit or change of form produced during the organism's life and affecting the body cells, as distinct from the germ cells, can be transmitted to these latter and so to succeeding generations. More recent experimenters have thrown some doubt upon Weissman's conclusion, and it appears possible that the Lamarkian factor may have to be given a place, though at most a minor one, along with natural selection as part of the mechanism of evolution.

There is a third factor in organic evolution, of which the validity cannot be doubted, known as sexual selection. This operates in two ways. Firstly, the males best equipped for overcoming their competitors for the females, survive and beget offspring rather than the less formidable and cunning, and secondly, the males which seem most attractive to the female, those with brighter plumage or with more elaborate methods of courtship, have a better chance of gaining her favours than the rest, and so of perpetuating their characters.

Secondary sexual characters arising in the first way are the antlers of deer and the manes of lions, which are nothing more than the result of natural selection operating within a particular species. Attributes arising in the second way are the brilliant colours of many birds, their skill in song and dance, and such fantastic plumage as that of the peacock and the lyre-bird. Here, in the course of evolution, the females have moulded their mates according to their preferences.

The very obvious fact that evolution cannot be wholly explained by the various theories which we have outlined, or by any combination of them, has led some to adopt a more or less mystical interpretation of life. The theory of Orthogenesis inclines in this direction, attributing to some forms a kind of inner necessity to develop along predetermined and straight lines. It is doubtful, however, whether teleological principles such as Orthogenesis, the Entelechy of Driesch or the *Elan Vital* of Bergson really add to our knowledge, except to show more clearly where that knowledge is deficient. Though stimulating, they can scarcely be said to explain what is at present, and perhaps will always be, so fascinating and mysterious, the inmost nature of the trajectory of life.

We have described in a few words some of the means whereby man has risen to pre-eminence in the animal world. Sometime between a million and two million years ago man was beginning to diverge from his simian relatives. Most probably he had led a life in the trees which gave rise to the opposable toe and thumb, and perhaps to a slight differentiation between hand and foot. When he left arboreal life and came to the ground, he appears to have walked much as the anthropoid apes do now, in a semi-erect position. Gradually he adopted a more upright posture, the foot lost its power of grasping, becoming a specialized locomotory organ, and the hand was left free for prehension. The importance of his abandonment of the quadrupedal life can scarcely be exaggerated. The hand is not a highly adapted instrument for running, swimming or flying; it retains its primitive pentadactylic form, and above all, the art of prehension has been learnt in the trees. Here, with the opposable thumb, we have that essential for tool using, the link, the connector which enables a man and his tool to act as one, the device for attaching an infinity of new limb-endings.

The occasional use by apes, even in their natural state, of such weapons as cocoa-nuts is well known. No doubt man also used as a tool anything ready to hand long before he could properly be termed man. The first tools were taken as they were found—a stone or a stick, hurriedly snatched up in time of battle perhaps, and as soon cast away. There was no fabrication and, at first, no deliberate selection. The search for a suitable weapon marks a second stage, a more definite prevision, the holding in mind of an idea. Then eventually came the crude fashioning of a tool, the trimming of a branch or the breaking of a stone to make a deadlier weapon. Man had then definitely commenced upon his human career, that of implement maker.

If the grasping hand was necessary to this development, the reasoning brain behind the hand, directing the choice and use of the tool, was even more important. As we have seen, there are already among the higher apes an appreciable degree of intelligence and relatively large brains. But man's brain is very much larger and more complex than theirs and his intelligence is correspondingly keener. By the natural selection of his more accomplished varieties and mutations, and perhaps, as some think, [3] by his own exertions, the bulk and quality of his brain gradually increased far beyond those of his simian relatives, the hand grew more sensitive, and he approached his present condition of intelligence and bodily organization.

As soon as certain men began to fight with artificial weapons their power and chances of survival increased enormously. Immediately they began to multiply rather than the more conservative groups; consequently their superior mental gifts and their tool-using traditions were perpetuated. No longer is bodily prowess the all-important factor in the evolution of man, but the cunning with which tools are made and used outweighs in survival value the brute strength of the body which wields them. And so it is that tools and weapons, themselves the product of intelligence, have contributed, up to a point, to the progressive evolution of intellectual power.

The advantages of the detached tool are very great. Bodily instruments are in their own way perfect devices for exploiting certain features of their environment; their possessors use these tools in a masterly fashion; there is no lack of skill nor of accuracy, and the instruments of the lowliest organism are far more subtle than the most subtle of human artefacts. In spite of all their merits these tools of the body have their disadvantages. The organism, having

---

3   Sir Arthur Dendy, *Evolutionary Biology,* 4th Ed, p. 451.

developed wonderful specialized organs, is irrevocably committed to them for life and to the one narrow way of living involved in their use. It has paid the price of specialization, it is at the mercy of its own restricted efficiency, it cannot adapt itself to a great variety of circumstances. If man, instead of seizing a flint stone in the hunt and throwing it away afterwards, had in the course of ages developed a similar bodily appendage, then the making and attachment of all other tools would have been impossible. He would be a fine hunter, but that alone. Never could he become a builder of houses, a painter of pictures, a maker of pots and pans and a million other things, the superb changeling, the Proteus among organisms. The outstanding advantage of the extra-corporeal instrument is that it can be taken up at will and as soon abandoned for another. It is as though a man could select a body appropriate to the exigencies of the moment, adopting what is, in effect, a new physical constitution appropriate to the business in hand. In a word, he is supremely adaptable. It may take a million years to provide an animal with a specialized organ for running or swimming or flying, but man, by artifice, adapts himself in a thousand ways from moment to moment.

The artefact which makes such a series of transformations possible is not less adapted to its environment than the living organ. Its function as an aid in the creature's life governs both its form and its material. At first, among the tools of primitive peoples, there was no great specialization; one tool answered a variety of purposes and differed little from other tools. The same flint that was used in warfare might be used also for cutting a branch from a tree, for slaying an animal as well as for dressing its hide. At length, by small degrees, tools diverged, each branch from its parent stem becoming progressively adapted to some particular function. One Jack-of-all-trades tool no longer suffices a man; he must have one or many corresponding to each of his increasingly various activities. So from the primitive box on wheels evolved the farm wagon, the war chariot, the coach of state, hackneys, broughams, hansoms, growlers and all the rest, each of them adapted to a special purpose while preserving the common ancestral principle. And all the wealth and variety of human instruments, adapted to all manner of circumstances, have arisen in a similar way from less specialized prototypes.

The tool must be adapted to the physical constitution of its user as well as to the exterior condition with which it deals. Thus at one end of the hammer is the wooden shaft shaped to the hand, at the other the head of iron to strike the object. Every tool that retains direct contact with man must be moulded to the requirements of his body; this is a limiting condition in the development of instruments. The suit of clothes may not be too fantastic, the sword and shield may not exceed a certain weight, and though there may be any number of gradations between the bed of Ware or the iron couch of Og and the cradle there is no exceeding these limits.

Again every instrument is adapted to the material out of which it is made. So important is this governing factor, that the history of artefacts is a reflection of the history of the discovery and appropriation of materials. Often the deficiencies of the available raw materials have delayed progress rather than any lack of inventiveness.

The working and use of stone was pushed as far as it could well go—Neolithic workmanship has never been surpassed in its own field—but brass and iron were needed as a basis for further progress. The economical production of large quantities of iron at the time of the Industrial Revolution no doubt contributed to the great advance in technical achievement which marked that period. For there are certain shapes and uses to which a material lends itself and beyond which it may not readily be taken. A certain proportion of length to breadth and width is suitable for a stone beam; this ratio increases for wood, and is greatest of all for iron and steel. Therefore the plan of a building is greatly influenced by the material for beams which is at the disposal of the designer. For some purposes, perhaps for one purpose only, a given substance may be suitable, while for other purposes a great number of materials will serve equally well, though the peculiar qualities of each will more or less affect the form of the instrument it builds.

In yet another way the shape and structure of a tool are determined—by the tools with which it is made. It will have, as it were, birth-marks. It will infallibly have the impress of the instruments employed in its generation. The bowl made by the sole action of the hand will differ from the product of the potter's wheel, the sawn plank from the adze-hewn, the cast nail from the drawn and the forged. The capacity of the means is always revealed in the end.

So the artificial object is no simple fact. It is fraught with many meanings and is the outcome of an infinity of influences. It is more or less deliberately adapted to the conditions upon which it is brought to bear, to the work it is intended to perform, to its user; and it is limited by its material, by the instruments used in its making and by those associated with it in its subsequent employment. In addition, it is the product of a society, and, as such, there enter into the manufacture and form and use of any tool a whole mass of traditions, a welter of cultural relations and restrictions. An artefact cannot be rightly understood, in our own no less than in primitive cultures, without continual reference to the customs of the guild or group of men who make it, the complex of tools of which it is part, and the entire nexus of religious, family, commercial, political and economic usages among which it appears.

All this may be summed up in a word: the tool is adapted, adapted in many ways to a manifold environment. How have artificial objects arrived at their present stage of adaptation, rivalling even that of the living organ? How have they become more and more complex? The answer is the same as to the question, how have organisms become more complex and more specialized? They have evolved. But artificial evolution is at once vastly different from the organic, and strangely similar. Let us see how it works.

The first tools were, as we have already noticed, made without hands, picked up and used as they were found. Later, how much later we cannot tell, the tool was probably chosen with care from a large number of possible alternatives. The third step was the shaping by hand of a tool, the fourth, the fabrication of one tool by the use of another. From that moment onwards every tool was the product of some tool, though there are unimportant exceptions, some of which appear today, as when a boy throws a stone. At this fourth stage it might be said with approximate truth *Omnia instrumenta ex instrumento,* to adapt the famous dictum of Virchow. And this statement has a double significance; first, that every artefact is fashioned by and therefore partially determined by others, bearing always their mark, and second, that it is made to a greater or less extent after the pattern of other tools. There is one heredity of form and function and another heredity of manufacture among all the works of man. Thus it is true to say of any machine, as of a great modern steamship or an automobile, that it is the product, and so registers the traces, of all the tools used directly and indirectly in its construction, and of the tools that made these, and so back and back to the tools that were gathered from the face of the earth a million or so years ago. An all-seeing observer might perceive in the form of that ship the palimpsests of an infinity of implements, an inexhaustible document of human fabrication. And it is also true that the steamship follows a specific form which may be seen in co-existent examples, and again, though modified, in the older paddle-steamer, and so receding by way of sailing ships and galleys, sometimes with great strides, sometimes gradually, back to the primitive canoes and coracles, which were themselves no doubt suggested by a floating tree.

An artefact has a specific form which it derives from its predecessors. But without variation there can be no evolution. Every hand-made tool differs slightly from every other; no two products, even when machine-made, are precisely alike. The primitive craftsman who sets out to make a drum or a spear-thrower, though he follows the tribal custom, has nevertheless a little latitude of practice. A chance configuration of the wood may suggest an unusual feature of no practical advantage, a slip of the hand may yield a club of unusual shape, by accident or fancy the head of a battle-axe may be set at a narrower angle, or the shape and number of its projections may be varied. Usually such deviations are insignificant, having no effect upon the evolution of the type. But very occasionally the craftsman turns out, more by chance than design, a tool which proves definitely superior to the rest. If the conditions are favourable to its survival the innovation will be adopted, founding a somewhat modified type which will in all probability supplant the older and so lead to technical advancement. [4]

Less often there occur more definite breaks from tradition, or free mutations, as they have been called by Dr. Harrison. [5] In modern times there have been many instances of such salutatory development. The evolution of the writing-pen was marked by abrupt changes when first the steel nib took the place of the quill, and again when the fountain-pen was introduced. And the substitution of pneumatic for solid tyres, and of hollow walls for solid walls, since they involve new principles, did not come about by slow degrees.

---

4   Since writing the above I have come across the following passage in Prof. Julian Huxley's *Essays of a Biologist*, p.36. 'The evolutionist can often gain valuable light on his subject, on what one may call the economics of the process, by turning to study the development of human inventions and machines. There, although the ways in which variations arise, and the way they are transmitted, are different from those of organic evolution, yet the type of 'pressure', the perpetual struggle, and the advantage of certain kinds of variation therein—these are in essence really similar.
5   Brit. Assoc. Report, 1930

They were mutations. Or, in earlier times, the addition of a wooden haft to the stone blade and the barbing of a fish-hook, were no doubt important modifications which arrived, not by scarcely perceptible improvements, but by an abrupt change.

Just as there can be no clear-cut line of demarcation between varieties and mutations, so the invention of an entirely new type and the founding of an entirely new line of instruments, cannot always be distinguished from a mutation within an existing type. For however epoch-making the invention, it always owes something to past human achievement. Thus, though the discovery of metals and their use were performances without precedent, the foundations were laid when men first learned how to make fire and how to make and use stone implements—without these accomplishments bronze and iron tools were impossible. Or again, though the arc-lamp of Sir Humphrey Davy was an entirely new departure, it was based upon the electrical researches of many scientists. Accident has played a great part in technical progress, though genius may aid good fortune and the intelligent application of a chance discovery lead to important results. On other occasions necessity is the mother of invention; a need is observed and patient experiments over a long period eventually yield an adequate solution. Generally, however, inventions of such origin are more firmly rooted in tradition and less revolutionary than those which, like the invention of fire making, because they are practically unforeseeable, can only emerge by accident.

So the evolution of instruments proceeds partly hap-hazard and almost by necessity, partly by intelligence. Both of these factors are usually involved when an old type of tool is made out of a new kind of material. Changes come about which are dictated more by the nature of the new material than by human intention. Inevitably the fresh medium gives rise to a gradual transformation. At first full advantage is not taken of its capacities. Though executed in bronze, many early implements are clearly following the pattern of their stone prototypes. Concrete buildings, even now, imitate those of brick and stone; only by degrees are the peculiar merits and limitations of this new-old building material beginning to assert their proper influence over the appearance and structure of buildings. But given time, the old form is modified almost out of recognition as more and more daring essays are made with the new medium. At last iron frees itself from the trammels of stone and wood, steel from those of iron, and ferro-concrete from those of steel, making possible in each case the free use of inherent qualities.

By putting a tool to some novel use, as well as making it out of some new substance, it is often fertilized, given as it were a new lease of energetic life, resulting sometimes in the splitting off of new varieties and mutations, in divergent evolution. The steam engine, once invented, was found to be as valuable for marine as for terrestrial locomotion, for the propulsion of hammers no less than for driving wheels. Or, to take an earlier example, the very disadvantages of the arch borrowed by the mediaeval guilds from the Roman and Romanesque tradition, were pressed into service. Its side-thrust, which had hitherto been the bane of builders, was, after the trial of many expedients, at last frankly accepted and met by the counterthrust of the flying buttress—itself an arch, a new application of an old device, an invention responsible in a large measure for the form of the Gothic cathedral.

Change of material and change of use are both frequently due to the diffusion of artefacts. An alien tool introduced into a community must undergo some modification of form and manufacture. Somewhat as a mountain dandelion differs from that of the low lying meadow, though both may be from seeds of one plant, so when a tool enters a new environment it changes in sympathy with a new culture, new traditions, new climate, new raw materials, new tool complexes. Contacts between peoples, whether consequent upon war, trade, travel or migration, tend towards a furtherance of technical achievement and a mutual interchange, with consequent modifications, of many artefacts.

The gradual change of climatic conditions, the modification of a society's environment by natural or artificial agency, or the migration of a people to a new territory—all these too have a great effect upon material culture. The ancestors of the Maori, when they went to New Zealand, tried at first to acclimatize there the paper mulberry, from the bark of which they used to make their clothing. This and other experiments proving failures, they finally adopted a plant called New Zealand flax for the purpose. [6] Similarly, the shortage of many materials in the countries involved in the Great War, led to the employment of a number of substitutes, accompanied by modifications of form.

---

6   R. U. Sayce, *Primitive Arts and Crafts*, p. 62

We have described some of the principal circumstances in which variations and mutations occur. There is a third manner in which tools and artefacts diverge from type, which we may call integration. [7] All our large and complex machines are syntheses of hundreds of devices, of which the prototypes were, in most cases, independent. A modern house may be looked upon as a unit instrument comprising many tools integrated together. Such parts of it as the furniture are but loosely associated with the whole, and may be removed without any permanent injury. Others, such as doors, plumbing, drains and the like, are, as one might say, organic components the loss of which will more seriously impair the efficiency of the dwelling. Even so denuded, the house will still serve as a shelter, but take away a pillar or a beam and the whole will collapse. Every intricate fabric is so built up of smaller instruments, which are relatively free, more or less dependent, or intimately worked into the structure of the whole. And many smaller tools are combinations of two or more previous tools. Our Canterbury-claw hammer is the result of a union between an instrument for driving nails, and one for extracting them, and the school-boy's 'knife', which includes everything from a screwdriver to a pair of scissors, is an excellent example of a less thorough combination of tools.

Integration has, in fact, been as responsible as any other factor for the evolution of the artificial. By this means tools have advanced from one order to another, and, though these stages are often difficult to disentangle, we can trace the two tendencies, which we may call

---

7   Dr. Harrison calls this process cross-mutation.

individuation and integration, running side by side throughout all the history of artefacts. Individuation is the development of a type, the improvement of a separate unit. Integration is the association, incomplete and temporary, or so thorough that two or more units of a lower order are merged and lose identity, of types within a unit of a higher order. But however they are joined together, the component parts must affect each other's form, each must be adapted to every other and to the whole.

We have, then, the designer, the craftsman, the inventor, and all the human and external agents which provide change in the artificial, presenting, from time to time, to society the products of their labour, inspiration or influence, namely, varieties, mutations and integrations. Not all are accepted. The community selects from among these only certain forms. There is here not a natural selection of natural organisms, but an artificial selection of artefacts, though the latter operation is no less drastic within its field than the former in its field. Again the most trivial-seeming lack of adaptation will send the candidate for survival to the wall, and the least notable improvement ensure a long and healthy existence. Related on every hand to a living and dead environment, the tool must be adjusted in every particular; deficiency in a minor respect may lead to a swift and sure extinction.

At first glance, artificial selection, and particularly of the inert object, is intelligent, a reasoned process. To a less extent than one might have expected is this the case. We have already seen that, especially in the earlier part of his history, the strife of man with his environment has favoured the men with the best implements and with the mental qualities which lead to invention. But this is merely natural selection applied to men and their artificial appendages. Within the tribe natural selection begins to give way to artificial selection. At first there is, no doubt, no clear reasoning about tools, and little more than a vague association of ideas. A weapon of one pattern kills more surely than one of another pattern; dipped in poison it may not only wound but slay an enemy. Perhaps the reason is never grasped—there is magic in the shape or in the liquid, therefore it must be used. Or some cunning individual may really devise by reasoning an instrument, and less enterprising generations that follow, losing sight of the intention underlying the form, ascribe efficacy to the wrong cause, and multiply the object for centuries after it has ceased to have any practical value whatsoever.

Building upon the foundations laid down by his predecessors, a man devises a new or partially new thing. If his invention is not to die with him he must impart his knowledge; if he would have recognition he must give his ideas material form. The difficulties in the path of the inventor are formidable even now. In earlier times they were, on the whole, much more so, though there have been occasions when the new thing was not necessarily abhorrent. More often, if we may judge by existing so-called primitives, almost everything had its religious or magical significance. This action was propitious, that unfavourable; this tool might be used only by men, that only by women; one operation might be performed only by the use of a particular tool, another might be executed in a variety of ways. On every hand there were taboos. In such a community the inventor was as likely to meet with a violent death as to be acclaimed a saviour. So it is probable that a slow and safe rate of change was the rule. Everything depends—depends still—upon the nature of beliefs, upon the trend of tradition; if the invention cut across hallowed prejudices or did not receive the sanction of the powerful it stood little chance of immediate acceptance.

Allowing, then, for such impediments to progress as the overwhelming power of custom and the almost universal fear of the new, we may say that, in general and in the face of great difficulties, artificial selection proceeds, not by the multiplication of artefacts in huge numbers and the destruction of all but a few of the most efficient, but by a more economical means, by the action of intelligence. Nature's method is by trial and error, man's is also by trial and error, but of a different kind. At once, without any need to give them material shape, he can pass any number of possible forms through the sieve of his mind, and select from them only a few which are to be made. What nature, with unlimited extravagance, does physically, man does mentally, after a different fashion and with a minimum of waste. But he has not altogether abandoned the older method. He cannot foresee every eventuality, so he brings to his aid the method of physical trial and error, testing actual artefacts in use, making tool after tool and rejecting most, finding whether this form or that material is preferable to another, learning by his failures as well as by his successes to build better and bigger as he adds to the wealth of individual and social experience.

It is a function of the intellect—the primary function according to Bergson—to make and use tools which supplement the body. Beneath all the adaptations arising from the relations between function, raw material, manufacturing processes and environment in all its aspects, is the working, however obscured, of this faculty, without which there can be no technical progress. For external circumstances determine up to a point the nature of the artefact; intelligence is exercised beyond this point. A man finds himself insufficiently protected against the cold. What can he do to overcome this disability? He may take much exercise, but he will be at the mercy of the weather as soon as he is tired. He may obtain the skins of animals or clothe himself with leaves or bark or flax. He may migrate to a warmer land, light a fire, or build a house that is insulated against extremes of temperature, and heat its atmosphere by means of coal or wood or electricity. Given the requisite physical and mental resources he may select from such solutions of his problem one appropriate under the circumstances, and then select again, from all the possible ways in which the required work may be carried out, the order and manner of his procedure. At every stage there is choice, but choice only between a limited number of possibilities. Always man must obey Nature to make use of her, but always there are alternative ways of doing so. Thus intelligence is free to choose between the courses with which it is presented, free to combine, dissect, build up and tear apart the data of sense and memory, and above all to construct out of such heterogeneous material plans for instruments of the body, which are reviewed, selected, and finally manufactured with the means at its disposal.

Life has risen from small and unpromising beginnings to forms of great complexity and power, and the methods by which this has come about are many and varied. Nature has a capacious sleeve from which she may produce at any moment some novel design, some unprecedented mode. It is not likely that her bag of tricks is near to exhaustion even yet. We often forget how recently she revolutionized her programme; within the last five or ten million years—a brief interval of geological time—there has been an extraordinary change in the material forms which she has used, no less than in the mental characters associated with these. There has been a parallel and related development of intellect and of artificial forms. Many preliminary essays involving the creation of artificial instruments were made, as we have noticed, long before man appeared, but when at last he arrives there exists a perfect medium for the realization of what was before little more than tentative experiment. 'Life, not content with producing organisms, would fain give them as an appendage inorganic matter itself, converted into an immense organ by the industry of the living being,' says Bergson. [8] The evolution of the organism, of its corporeal instruments and their uses, having attained a level where the rudiments of intelligence and a suitable bodily organisation occur together, changes its character. The body of a man is now the live core, around which is gathered a rapidly evolving corpus of artificial organs that, considered in their entirety,

---

8   *Creative Evolution*, p. 170.

enwrap the world. If the parasite, in the last resort, cannot be looked upon as complete without its host, the spider without its web, or the bee without its flowers, neither can a man ultimately be regarded as entire, as a fully equipped individual, without his complement of artificial organs. [9] His living body changes little in ten thousand years, but within this period his extended 'body' has grown and altered till he is become, in effect, a wholly different animal. His effectiveness in the world has increased many-fold; his relations to all life and inert things have been changed utterly; he differs more from proto-man, in this sense, than the latter differed from the least of mammals. He has become, in this sense alone, another species; even he constitutes, one is tempted to say, the only representative of a new order while remaining, in the orthodox sense, but little changed from the stock whence he came.

Here, at the periphery, man evolves with a swiftness that is unknown in the rest of nature. Further, he directs, even if his control is partial and faltering, his extra-corporeal evolution. In the role of Life's most accomplished child, he has, as it were, been entrusted with this branch of her many enterprises. Using man as her vicegerent, Life has made a great venture. Working through him and on his account, she has added to the ancient protoplasmic cell-forms vast ramifying 'organs' of wood, stone, iron, steel, and a thousand other once-'alive' or always-'dead' materials, which are used, no less effectively because they are not interpenetrated with her subtle processes, to build along with the cells a kind of composite organism which will subdue the

9   See Chapter IV for the further discussion of this problem.

rest of creatures, improve by exercise the intelligence which is at the root of it all, and crown the whole hierarchy of life. Coarse metal and stone take on significant shape by virtue of the workings of the delicate cellular units, creating continually from the uncontrolled world another world, tamed, pressed into the immediate service of Life, a world with the breath of Life breathed upon it, rather than into it.

But we may not anticipate too much our conclusions; we must return to our more detailed survey of artificial evolution. So far we have noted the more important factors involved. While taking care not to over-emphasize the analogies between organic and artificial evolution, and to under-estimate their differences, it is impossible to disregard the fact that the development of artefacts bears at many points a striking resemblance to the development of living organisms. And, as we proceed now to trace briefly some developments in the history of the rise and decline of instruments, further similarities will appear, reminding us again of the fact that, though we are dealing with 'inorganic', it is Life itself which has made of such stuff organs for herself.

Let us turn to the most primitive instruments. Somewhat as the early organisms, judging by the Protista now living, were *relatively* simple in structure and unspecialized, differing far less from the non-living than do the higher animals and plants, and were exceedingly prolific, so the eoliths of primitive man bear little evidence of the potentialities of the external organ; often they can hardly be distinguished from the unworked stone; they are simple and unspecialized and were, as a rule, made in great numbers with little trouble, soon to be replaced after a short term of usefulness. As the tool's parts become more numerous and more differentiated from each other, and its materials are brought together from more varied sources, the tool takes longer to make, is more expensive, and is generally expected to give longer service. Sticks and stones can be shaped rapidly, thrown aside and replaced with the greatest of ease. But the more complex and elaborate the machine, the less likely it is to be abandoned early in its career, the more efficient are the devices for its protection, and the longer are the intervals between the production of similar machines. While many kinds of tools progress consistently, there remain others which have scarcely changed in character, though their manufacture has usually been modified. Nails and pins, bricks and brick and mortar walls, wooden beams and a thousand other articles of use are now much as they were centuries ago; only their uses have been changed a little and the larger units to which they belong a great deal. Like unicellular organisms, they persist side by side with those higher and less prolific types that now occupy the centre of the stage.

The general trend of evolution is towards complexity, efficiency and the reduction of waste. But neither vital nor artificial evolution leads necessarily to the advancement of powers; often there is a falling off, some or all of the parts losing their old effectiveness, and the whole becomes 'degenerate'. It is as though an artefact gathers a momentum during its period of material usefulness, which often carries it beyond the point where it ceases to have any other value than that conferred by the human emotions. It has become worked into the substance of a tradition which changes but slowly and cannot keep pace with material invention. So, many tools, after their heyday of functional activity is over, eke out a protracted old age as symbols, mere shadows of the past and their former selves, with failing or lost powers, and often with a beauty which makes for their preservation for an indefinite period. The mace, richly decorated and useless, remains as a symbol of an authority which is now upheld by means of much deadlier weapons. The sword still lingers on even in the day of the gas-bomb. It is in association with religious and political ritual, where the effect rests upon ancient custom and picturesque observances rather than upon mere efficiency or intellectual appeal, that we find, enriched and debased, some of the ancient instruments of the race.

There are many other ways in which types are preserved for their own sake. The toys of children include both altered examples of older artefacts and simplified or miniature reproductions of older ones. Among primitive peoples, charms and fetishes, as well as personal ornaments and offerings to the dead, consist in many cases of diminished or otherwise modified reproductions of articles which have had or still possess practical uses. One of the most interesting processes by which an artefact may degenerate and at the same time acquire another use is by serving as currency. Unworked iron suitable for making axe blades, knives, and other implements, is used as a medium of exchange in many African tribes, but in some instances the natives are not content with such serviceable currency and work the iron into 'show' money—curious and impractical spears and axes which are displayed on ceremonial occasions and for the ostentation of wealth. [10] Again, the Torres Straights Islanders used formerly to give to the young brides fish-hooks which were of the utmost practical value. Now, these presents bear only a remote resemblance to the original hook and are worn on the back as ornaments. Only a few, however, of all the tools which have become useless can find a place among the pensioners; most disappear. There is a merciless struggle for existence among our artefacts. At any moment one may be threatened by another that is in some way better adapted; a variation or a mutation may at one blow put many tools out of action for ever. They may linger on a little while like the horse-drawn cart and the sailing ship, but, like organisms that are on the way to extinction, every year sees a decline in their numbers. Or, to take a different kind of example, nowhere is the struggle among instruments seen more vividly than in a great American city, where the race for light and air between the sky-scrapers resembles strikingly the competition between the trees of a densely wooded forest to gain the upper light.

Sometimes whole instruments fall into decay, at other times there is an atrophy of certain parts. Portions become superfluous, while others continue to function and progress. The redundant features are often retained as 'vestigial organs', somewhat as the whale carries the much diminished and quite useless vestiges of the hind limbs which it once possessed. Samuel Butler drew attention to this parallel between tools and organisms, giving as an example the persistence of a rim

---

10   Leo Frobenius, *Childhood of Man*, p. 450.

at the base of a pipe bowl, though it had long ceased to have any other than an ornamental function. [11] So also for a long time railway carriages and automobiles continued to retain some of the trappings of the coach from which they were both derived, and many of the most up-to-date saloon cars have still the arm, jointed apparently but not in fact, which was once employed in the folding of the collapsible hood. Vestiges like this persist for centuries as embellishments upon all kinds of useful articles, and above all in architecture—that most conservative of arts. Perrot and Chipiez held that the Doric Order, with its tryglyphs, mutules and guttae, was derived from the timber palaces of Mycenae. Even today, architects of the classical school multiply these details which, though they have had no structural value for more than three thousand years, still retain evidences of their utilitarian origin.

Such forms, translated from one material to another, are called skeuomorphs. When a new raw material is employed in the making of an article the features of the old craft tend to be carried over, despite the fact that the new medium has rendered them obsolete. The primitive utensils supplied by nature—shells, horns, bones, gourds and nut-shells, are sometimes copied by primitive folk in their pottery and basketwork with very little modification of form; or the characteristics survive as surface decoration, as when a pottery vessel is painted with a pattern imitating basketry or leather-work, the older lashing of a spear-head is copied in bronze, or a jar is ornamented with the outline of a carrying-net. Men become accustomed to the

---

11   *Note Books,* 1913 ed., p. 47

established appearances and avoid a sudden change if they are able. In addition, there is always an interval between the first employment of a new medium and the complete mastery of its technique, and it is during this period of transition that skeuomorphic design is so frequently to be found.

Divergent evolution, both of organisms and artefacts, is favoured by isolation. Where an island has been long cut off from the mainland, or impassable mountains and other physical barriers have severed the connection of a species with its parent stock, the differences of environment, and perhaps the peculiar inherent qualities of the branch type, have led to its divergence. Accordingly, in isolated areas, many remarkable artefacts and organisms are to be found, and ancient forms that have been protected from the struggle which would ensue if they were to come into contact with more advanced types. The ocean barriers between the Old and the New Worlds and Australasia were responsible for the great differences which have arisen between the organisms of the three great land masses, and responsible too for the divergence of human cultures with their artefacts. Especially in Australia there survive many archaic forms, such as the marsupials, the platypus and the spiny anteater among mammals, and primitive tribes with many peculiar implements and customs. But modern means of communication tend gradually to do away with cultural isolation; human life with its material aids tends increasingly to conform to a universal standard, modified only to suit the various local conditions. The older ways and means are no longer sheltered but brought face to face with their modern competitors. Primitive handicrafts disappear before the cheaper machine-made wares; textiles from Manchester and Tokyo replace the products of the hand-looms; the petrol-can supplants the pottery vessel; and rifles, iron hammers and steel axes and knives render the cunning of the flint-knapper of no avail. Eventually these relics of the past will be found with the Dinosaurs and the Trilobites only in our museums. An invention or discovery made here today is blazed across the world tomorrow, and in a little while established everywhere; the forms upon which it improves are already doomed, though execution of sentence may be postponed indefinitely.

If we were to set ourselves the task of tracing the phylogeny of one series back from the present into the recent past, and further, if we could, to its obscure beginnings, we should find that though we could often make out a typological series, indicating a well marked linear development, there would appear at frequent intervals occurrences having no parallel in organic evolution. In view of the profound differences between the organism and its artefact, this might well be expected. The tool may quite suddenly be made from a material not hitherto employed; it may as suddenly lose a part, become enormously increased or diminished in size, or have grafted upon it a feature derived from a type that has no near relation to it. From time to time the histories of tools intertwine, merge, drift apart or become lost in one another, in a way that is unparalleled in nature. There is in artifice far more latitude of operation. No tools so removed in character from one another but what may be combined; none so complex but what their whole constitution may be recast almost over-night.

Mr. R. U. Sayce has sketched the development of a series of stringed instruments, commencing with the bow which was used by the Bushmen to produce one sound, followed by a number of bows used at once and by a bow with several strings, to give a variety of notes. To such an instrument a resonator has been added by several African tribes. So arose the 'West African harp'—seven bows fitted onto a wooden sound-box. From this point there is a bifurcation in the series: on the one hand the lyre is developed, where the strings are attached to a horizontal bar, and, on the other hand, the harp is improved by the addition of pegs for tightening the strings, a front pillar is introduced, and finally the instrument is placed in a case and the strings are no longer plucked but struck with hammers, as in the harpsichord and the modern piano. [12] As Mr Sayce points out, his examples have been taken from many cultures and belong to different periods, and simplicity may by no means imply antiquity. Nevertheless, the evolution of this type of instrument has no doubt followed a course similar to that outlined.

In the development of such a series it is easy to see how far-reaching may be the modifications in size, form, material, and even in function, and how abruptly they may occur, whereas the most violent of mutations amongst organisms can compass, so far as evidence goes to show, only a relatively small change. And this is due in no small measure to the fact that intelligence has to do with a very different

---

12   *Primitive Arts and Crafts,* p. 105, et seq.

kind of material from Life's intricate structures. There is, in fact, but little resemblance between an organism and any machine that we have yet made. The disparity between what Sir Thomas Browne called the 'mathematicks' of the human body, and the clash of iron, steel, wood and rubber, is as obvious as the disparity between the means by which artificial and organic evolution have come about.

Again, that the growth of an individual machine is the very antithesis of the growth of an organism is so obvious as to need no more than a brief mention here. The first is no more than a moulding of parts, outside and severally, according to a plan, and their assembly afterwards. A machine does not, in the truer sense, grow at all; it arrives when its parts are joined together, but the organism grows from within; its body is the mechanism for its own growth. Given the requisite environment, the fertilized cell bears within itself the capacity to build up, out of the raw material which it has made its own, the infinitely complex creature of millions of cells.

A machine does not grow, neither, in any ordinary sense, can it reproduce its kind. It is unlikely that, even if industrialism survives for many centuries, men will ever see a fertile union between a pair of steam engines, as Butler playfully prophesied, or tiny locomotives gambolling in front of the engine shed. But, as we have noticed, tools of some kind are almost invariably used in the construction of machines and implements; these tools are, in some sort, the progenitors of the machine, though they are usually of an entirely different character from their product. A factory, the purpose of which is to manufacture locomotives, would be better regarded as a specialized social organ for that end.

The essence of life lies in the instability of its materials; it is always balanced upon a fine edge. The parts of a machine tend to be stable. And, though means for its self-repair and automatic adjustment to a few circumstances have been devised, and no doubt will be improved upon, a machine responds effectively to only a few changes in its environment, and without attention will very soon cease to function. However we view them, it would be a mistake to regard man's works as having any intrinsic qualities which are more than superficially analogous to those of organisms. The peculiar value of the artificial object consists precisely in its essentially different constitution from that of the living organ, on the one hand, and in its essentially homologous function on the other hand. The external organ is not made after the pattern of the internal. To be of most service to life it must have qualities which do not appear in the organism. The limitations of material and function, the conservatism of Life's older methods of reproduction, the slowness of her changes and her waste—all are overcome by the crude but invaluable organ made by artifice. The live spot remains at the centre, but its effectiveness is multiplied a thousand-fold by the fact that it is enclosed within, and works by means of, an ever growing circle of 'dead' organs that are different from itself—in a word, the artificial world.

..............when to my car
my money yokes six spankers, are
their limbs not my limbs? Is't not I
on the proud racehorse that dash by?
Mine all the forces I combine,
the four-and-twenty legs are mine!

Faust, Anster's translation

CHAPTER IV

The Instruments of the Individual

In our last chapter the tool has been called an *extension* of the body that uses it, an extra-corporeal organ. It is time to state more definitely what is meant by this. The question may no longer be put off—what, then, is an individual? In what sense can it be said that an individual's body is extensible? You might object: is it not clear that the limits of a man's body are strictly defined, and that his tools are nothing but special features of his environment, no more part of him, in fact, than the earth on which he walks and the air around him?

To these questions we must seek an answer in this chapter, but first let us hear what others have said about the artificial instrument and the body.

It was Samuel Butler, the philosopher whom people refused to take seriously, who first had much to say upon the subject. One quotation will suffice: 'They (machines) are to be regarded as the mode of development by which human organism is most especially advancing, and every fresh invention is to be considered as an additional member of the resources of the human body... By the institutions and stage of science under which a man is born it is determined whether he shall have the limbs of an Australian savage or those of a nineteenth century Englishman. The former is supplemented with little save a rug and a javelin; the latter varies his physique with the changes of the season, with age, and with advancing or decreasing wealth. If it is wet he is furnished with an organ which is called an umbrella and which seems designed for the purpose of either protecting his clothes or his lungs from the injurious effects of rain. His watch is of more importance to him than a good deal of his hair, at any rate than of his whiskers; besides this he carries a knife, and generally a pencil case. His memory goes in a pocket book. He grows more complex as he becomes older and he will then be seen with a pair of spectacles, perhaps also with false teeth and a wig; but, if he be a really well-developed specimen of the race, he will be furnished with a large box upon wheels, two horses and a coachman.' [1] Long before Butler, Giordano Bruno had the quaint notion: 'Thy boots and spurs live, when thy feet carry them; thy hat lives when thy head is in it; and so the stable lives when it contains the horse or mule, or even yourself.' Bergson, speaking of the Great War, has said: 'Each new machine being for man a new organ—an artificial organ which merely prolongs the natural organs—his body became suddenly and prodigiously increased in size, without his soul being able at the same time to dilate to the dimensions of his new body.' [2] Among biologists, Julian Huxley has pointed out that Life, having produced the human brain with its powers, releases the individual 'from waiting servile upon substance. Now to its own size it can add the size of all its tools and machines—by them now is measured the range of its action.' [3]

---

1   *Note Books*, 1913 ed. pp. 50-51.
2   *Paroles Francaises*, 2nd series. (Eng. Trans., Hibbert Journal, 1915, pp. 473-474.
3   *The Individual in the Animal Kingdom*, p. 29

And Sir Arthur Dendy: 'A railway train or an aeroplane is no less an organ of locomotion than an arm or a wing; a drainage system is an organ of excretion; a telescope is an organ of vision and telegraphic or telephonic apparatus is nothing more nor less than a nervous system shared by the community.'

But if tools and bodily aids of all kinds are indeed extensions of the body, what are the boundaries set to the individual's bodily organization? In the last resort all, or nearly all, the tools in the world operate for his benefit, and not only these but men also are his organs of life. We have arrived at an apparently impossible situation, where every edge is blurred and all is nebulous, a paradoxical world which common-sense refuses to take seriously. Let us examine a little more closely this notion of bodily individuality about which men seem to be so certain.

Taken in the broadest sense of the word, individuality is a category fundamental to our thinking; in fact, according to Locke, 'the *principium individuationis* is existence itself.' In thought we isolate things. The object of contemplation is silhouetted against the background of other things, thrown up against its *milieu*. And because an object cannot be considered except in relation to its setting, because to exist at all it must interact with an environment, it is never complete in itself, an absolute individual, an isolated object, unless indeed we call the Universe or God the only perfect individual. Ordinarily, when we speak of a body we necessarily limit it, sever it from its field. But this is a highly arbitrary operation; actually, in a manner of speaking, the body exists wherever it exerts influence, and, in the final analysis 'everything is everywhere at all times,' as Whitehead has said. Strictly, no individual has any boundaries either of space or time save those of the universe. But it is a function of our minds to perceive clearly only the immediate pattern of an object; to this pattern we give the name of individual, and the degree of its individuality is the degree of its independence of the background.

Viewed in its internal relations, an individual is a system of parts which are, in the wide sense, *organised;* that is to say, they are unlike one another and enter into complex mutual relations, so constituting together a new whole.

To make clearer the relations of part to whole and to other parts, we will consider a few examples. Take first an ordinary pebble. In practice we should regard it as a clearly defined unit, circumscribed by its rounded surface. Actually it affects every other particle of matter in the universe, however slightly; its presence, it might be said, is felt everywhere. For example, its particles exercise gravitational attraction upon all other particles; there is a universal tendency for all bodies to move towards the pebble. These external forces are really no less a part of it than its internal forces or its 'matter', which modern physics has robbed of its 'materiality'. From the internal aspect the pebble is composed of parts, some lying on the periphery, some within. The former are brought under the influences differing somewhat from those affecting the latter; the surface parts reflect and absorb light, sustain wear, and gain and lose heat more readily than do the interior particles. The various stresses set up within the material of the pebble by different agencies, are by no means evenly distributed. There is, in short, some division of labour—to borrow a term from the economists—among the parts of the stone. But break the pebble into half-a-dozen fragments. Have the pieces lost any of the essential characters of the original? It is true they are not rounded and weathered; they are smaller and angular, but they have lost none of the stoniness. Divide a stone and you have stones, objects of the same order, organised to the same degree though not in precisely the same manner. We have here, then, a very low order of wholeness, a rudimentary, but none the less actual, differentiation of parts. But as soon as the stone is broken each fragment is equipped with its complement of differentiated particles.

Now consider such a tool as an axe, with its stone blade, lashings of sinew and wooden haft. Here are definitely heterogeneous parts, mutually adapted portions which are of different materials and forms; each part stands in more or less constant relation to the others, and has its proper function when the tool is used. The handle for grasping, the blade for cutting, and the lashing for binding these—each is necessary to the whole and has its place which the other parts could not fill, in the economy of the instrument. Take away one of them or break the axe into fragments and you will not have a number of miniature axes, as we had smaller stones, but useless debris. The axe is *organised*. It is, in the broadest sense, an individual; it cannot be divided without losing its 'axe-ness'.

When we examine a much more complex tool, an aeroplane, for instance, we find these properties to a greater degree. The parts are far more elaborately organized, their mutual relations are far more complex, the integrity of the machine relies upon a far more thorough division of labour among more numerous and more diverse 'organs'.

The aeroplane has greater pretensions to individuality than has the axe. But the aeroplane, like any other tool, has its field. In particular, it is both dependent upon and influences pilot, mechanic, petrol, the air and the world in general. Ultimately, it is not entire within the familiar limits of engine and wings and body; it is dependent upon a host of influences and affects to some degree the whole of things.

But it is to the living organism that the words 'individual' and 'organised' are most applicable and for which they are as a rule reserved. The 'lowest' creatures of which we have knowledge, the unicellular animals and plants, have parts which are differentiated in function and form, and though under certain conditions the resultant portions may survive artificial division, there is always a temporary disorganization, a loss of efficiency, when a part is severed from the whole. The behaviour of the component parts of the organism can be understood only when viewed as contributing to the plan of the whole. By the existence of an internal principle of unity, heterogeneous parts subserve the general well-being and the dependence of each part is maintained. The result of these inward relations is that the organism as a whole fends for itself in the world, where it has a measure of independence. Thus we may certainly call an Amoeba, for example, an individual, more complete and of a far higher order than an aeroplane, for its dependence upon the world is less immediate and it makes shift for itself and its species.

As soon as we come to consider a colony of cells, however, such as the microscopic Pandorina, we are landed in difficulties. The colony consists of sixteen cells embedded in a gelatinous envelope, each with its pair of flagella projecting from the surface of the mass. There is no division of labour between the individual cells; each gets its own living, feeds by itself, and multiplies by division into sixteen daughter cells, forming thus a new colony which severs its connection with the others. Doubtless some advantages are gained by this unspecialized association, but the Pandorina colony cannot be regarded as a true individual; at least such individual definiteness as it has is imposed from outside; it has but a rudimentary internal principle of unity.

Between Pandorina and the most elaborately organized vertebrate, there can be arranged a graded series of organisms which show more and more division of labour between their cells and organs. At no stage in this series can we say: here is a true individual, before there were only colonies, mere aggregates. In the evolution of the Metazoa individuation does not arise suddenly. Its beginnings are seen in Pandorina and Gonium, and it progresses *pari passu* with, first, the mutual dependence of the organism's parts, and, second, with the independence of the organism as a whole. For individuality is a matter of degree.

Volvox is a minute colony of many thousands of cells connected by fine strands of protoplasm and arranged in the form of a hollow sphere. Most of the cells are similar and are provided with flagella which propel the colony through the fresh water in which it lives; but there are other larger non-flagellate cells whose business it is to reproduce the colony. So we must allow Volvox to have a greater degree of individuality than Pandorina, since there is a division of labour amongst its cells and a corresponding mutual dependence. It is an individual of the second order comprising individuals of the first order.

Once cells have become permanently associated and a system of mutual aid arises between them, the basis has been provided for the evolution of types where ever more complete specialization exists among an increasing number of cells. The trend of evolution is to improve the type, up to a point, by individuation. It is unnecessary for us to trace the immense number of intermediate stages between Volvox and the vertebrates, with their many kinds of cells, tissues and organs. It is sufficient to notice that the individuality of the multicellular organism tends to progress at the expense of the individuality of its cells; the more specialized and various the latter, the more various are the functions and the more marked the individuality of the resultant organism.

But there are many ways in which the individuality of even the highest of organisms is incomplete, reminding us again that we have to do with a principle that is never absolute. Many diseases are due to an insubordination among some of the cells of the body, which have lapsed from the control of the whole. Again certain cells in the animal body, such as the spermatozoa and the leucocytes, or white blood corpuscles, have a considerable degree of independence. These corpuscles behave much as the Amoeba; they devour minute organisms which have found their way into the body; they can pass through the walls of blood-capillaries and can be kept alive outside the body for a short time under suitable conditions. These cells have not entirely surrendered their individuality to that of the animal to which they belong. And what of the individuality of Siamese twins and of monsters more completely joined? When a revolutionary metamorphosis takes place in the history of an insect and in many other lives, is every stage a distinct individual, or the life cycle of several very different forms? Are the alga and the fungus that comprise the lichen two or one? Is the plant, which sends out suckers that take root and yet remain joined to the parent plant, one or many? And is there not an individuality of the species, of Life itself? These are all questions which must be approached in the light of our two criteria of individuality—internal and external dependence or independence—but to which there can be found no definitive answers. [4]

How does the foregoing illuminate the relations between man and his artificial works? Since it possesses a complex structure, the higher animal is able to perform many diverse actions; the more efficient its bodily tools and the more various their functions, the greater, as a rule, is the independence of the animal. Now a man, by relying upon his extra-corporeal tools, has endowed himself with a far greater number of powers. He has added a host of highly specialized instruments to his own, and these have increased immensely his independence of nature; *taken with them* his organic individuality is far greater than that of any other animal. Between him and them there is now a thorough mutual dependence; by them he lives, subdues nature, feeds, keeps warm, fights, builds, destroys; by him they are devised, multiplied, controlled, tended with solicitous care. And wherever there is such a mutual dependence among objects, there we find arising a new individual. Gaining individuality on the

---

4   The idea of individuality also involves a degree of permanence, a temporal continuity, and raises many other questions for which we have no space here.

one hand, man must lose it to some extent on the other; he cannot be independent of both nature and of artificial instruments. He has to make his choice. But dependence upon his own tools, so long as he has them well in hand, is the road of increasing individuality. For corresponding to the functions of the man-plus-instruments is the intelligence of the man, his diverse states of mind, which are the psychological counterpart of his extended artificial apparatus. A man's body, in effect, is part 'natural', part 'artificial'; one part he has received as the legacy from the long line of his animal ancestors, and the other he—or rather the race—has created and maintains and dominates by the operation of intelligence.

But it must be remembered that we have to do with a tendency, with degrees of individuality, not with something that is actually realized. The mutual dependence of tool and man, so complete in many ways, falls short in others. In very favourable climates where food is abundant, it would no doubt be possible for a man to live for a space without artificial aids, though his life would be utterly different from that of the meanest savage. Man does not yet differ so utterly from his simian ancestors that he would be unable under all circumstances to exist for a little while without his tools. His dependence upon these for the bare necessities of existence has not yet proceeded so far, though he owes all, or nearly all, that is over and above mere existence to the artificial. Then, because body and instrument are not physically continuous, any amount of substitution of either may take place without much loss of efficiency. Any machine of the right pattern will suffice me, and from the machine's standpoint, if it may be said to have one, anyone with sufficient skill will serve to minister to its needs. So when a tool of mine is injured the damage is as a rule easily restored, my impaired organization is soon mended. And there is, of course, that most important distinction between the living tools and the dead: the former develop together from the original fertilized cell; whereas the latter are added from outside; they are neither born nor die with a man, the term of their existence lies apart from his life-span, and they may belong to another or to a thousand others no less than to himself.

These reservations and distinctions do not at all invalidate our general claim, but, after all, the inclusion of his tools within man's bodily individuality is only one of several possible interpretations of the facts. It would be perfectly reasonable, for instance, to look upon the man as the instrument of his machine, just as in any other co-operative union, such as that between the ants and their useful guests, either party may be regarded as the tool of the other. It all depends upon whose side we choose to take; quite legitimately we usually describe the partnership from the point of view of the dominant member, but there is an obverse as well as a reverse side to the situation. If we think of the first tools, flint-stones, sticks, and such small and simple things, it seems ridiculous to make the man the instrument of his tool, but the sight of our modern colossi, tended by thousands of relatively tiny creatures, carefully groomed and victualled and doctored by their faithful attendants, cannot fail to impress one with the insignificance of the puny animals crawling around and within them. In bulk, in economic importance, in the care and attention which is bestowed upon it, the great machine far surpasses its 'master'. Often it is a kind of Juggernaut which occasionally takes its toll of human lives, demands willing and unwilling service, and is not without serious mental and physical effects upon its servitors. The term machine-slave has passed into our language, and expresses a fact, even if, like most truths, it is really a half-truth or something less.

But the anthropocentric view of tools as bodily extensions is clearly justified because man is, in spite of such indications to the contrary, the controlling, the dominant partner, and though his tools affect somewhat his physical constitution, he is responsible for every detail of their design, with the exception, of course, of the animals and plants which he has taken into service. Machines are artificial; they are human creations. If one day they should become as nature, as things not perfectly understood nor perfectly adjusted to man's requirements, then, and then only would he surrender to them his position in the partnership, and become a mere adjunct of the machine, a part of its mechanism. Some believe that such a state of affairs is fast arriving, and there are certainly indications that some very decisive measures will have to be taken if man is to use his machines for the general good. It will before long be necessary to adapt more thoroughly our slow-moving economic system to the swift evolution of technics.

As with all other creatures, there are no definite limits set to the physical organization of a man; ultimately he includes the world. But those parts of his so-called environment upon which he is more directly dependent, and with which he is more permanently associated, are the *fringe* of his bodily organization. As he, and these instruments which are gathered around him, become more and more mutually dependent, they tend to become part of him. It is as though, organically considered, the individual were first and foremost a live body, less—far less—the artificial aids outside, and sometimes within, that body, and still less the untouched world beyond, upon which, nevertheless, the man is still ultimately dependent. Schematically, the situation may be indicated by a series of concentric spheres,

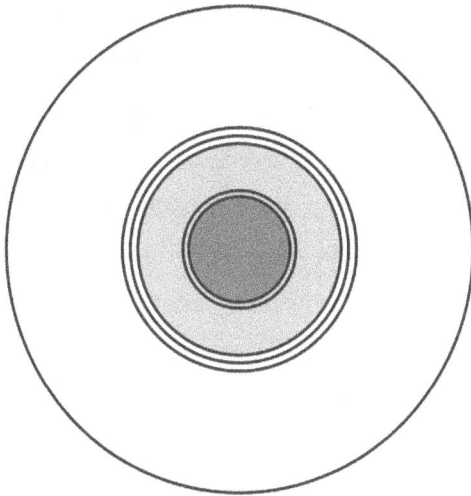

of which the innermost represents the body. Even to this we cannot give a definite outline; it shades off into the environment. Enclosing the body is the sphere of its instruments, again without a clear-cut boundary but merging into the outermost region, the world, which is nothing but the instrument of the innermost spheres, the scheme of things upon which man-plus-tools, no less than the meanest plant, is entirely dependent.

In the second chapter we saw that there were three courses, with an infinite number of compromises lying between them, open to the living organism. First, it may become so adapted as to be able to use the world at large as the instrument of its life, and direct minister to its needs. This is the way of the vegetable. It is at the mercy of its environment, governed entirely by circumstance, immediately dependent. Then there is the way of the parasite, which is also highly adapted to a ready-made environment; but it employs as its direct instrument, not nature *in toto,* but the body of another organism. The third course is to do what man has done and what certain other animals have begun to do, to enlarge itself, to create around its living body a system of instruments which take over, to a great degree, the functions of the bodily ones. Precisely like the vegetable, man has become so modified that he is able to make the raw influences of the world his servants. But he does this principally by the adaptation of his external organs. Onto them he has shifted the brunt of the specialization necessary to harness nature. He *and his tools* are not a whit less dependent upon the world, but he—and this is the way of increasing individuality—preserves himself from the direct dependence of the plant by relying upon his artificial instruments, over which he has a large measure of control.

It is interesting to notice how language and everyday thought bear out the fact that a man's property and clothes are, in a sense, part of him. We come to think of the clothes of our acquaintances as extensions of themselves. The clothes, it is said, make the man. They express his nature. They are often a valuable guide to the sort of person he is. Bowler hat and pin-striped trousers; black trilby, flannel 'bags' and a woollen tie; the immaculate, well-fitting and well-carried suit with every detail carefully attended to—these are indications of the quality of a man, far more socially relevant than a good deal of what is a part of the living body. We say: I am poor, meaning of course that one's available extensions are poor in number or quality; or, colloquially: he stung me, implying that one has lost money; or again we scold a child for having dirtied himself, when it is his clothes that are soiled.

Our estimate of a man is never confined to a judgment of his living body and its behaviour. His possessions, servants, house and wealth are all taken into account, and not unreasonably. Kings and tramps, millionaires and paupers, prime ministers and scavengers, are appraised, whether we desire it to be so or not, according to the measure of their property, the facilities they have for extension. Their power inevitably impresses us somewhat, or their weakness disparages, and power is really extension. The man surrounded with luxury is quite truly a 'well-developed specimen of the race', that is of the race of man-plus-instruments. And often men have more regard for their property than for their living bodies, sacrificing health for gain, which is a kind of possession-health.

Tools as well as organisms lend themselves to a system of classification; there is a typology of artefacts corresponding to a taxonomy of organisms. There are many possible ways of classifying instruments, but for our purpose it is convenient to arrange them according to function rather than form, according to their purpose rather than their shape or material. This we shall do very briefly, and chiefly to illustrate the conclusions of the first part of this chapter.

We may distinguish seven principal types of inanimate tool:-

Those for supplementing or replacing

1. The hand and the arm—implements for fabrication.

2. The legs—means of locomotion.

3. The natural integuments—clothes and buildings

4. The digestive and excretory organs—food-factories, kitchens, drains, etc.

5. Other organs—the accessories of the orthopaedist.

6. The organs of sight.

7. The organs of hearing. The brain.

This, or any other scheme of types so involved, cannot pretend to any accuracy; some tools will be included under more than one heading, and the allocation of others may present difficulties, nevertheless it is sufficiently workable. We will review the development of each series in turn, remembering, of course, that in fact there has been no such separate evolution, but that each has to some extent affected the others. And we will avoid wearisome catalogues of tools that are, after all, perfectly familiar to most of us.

1. The hand, feeble, soft and small, is in itself a poor thing, capable of performing but a few weak actions, of which grasping is by far the most important. For striking powerful blows or cutting obdurate substances it is altogether unsuitable. Then rough flints of a few shapes and a few sticks are held in it, and already we have the point for boring, the wedge for cutting and hacking, the percussive hammer and the club, chisels and scrapers, the lever and the missile weapon—a veritable metamorphosis. By grinding and polishing, by the multiplication of types and the judicious selection of materials and natural objects, Neolithic man advanced far; nevertheless a field with immense possibilities was closed to him till copper, bronze and iron were available. In spite of this handicap, examples belonging to

the three kinds of 'hand' tool are to be found among peoples that, until recently, have had no metals. First there is the implement proper, held in the hand and used directly. This type merges by imperceptible degrees into the simple mechanical contrivance, where the energy supplied by the user undergoes some modification, is converted into a more useful form. In this class are the bow, the bow-drill, the grind-stone and, later, the pulley and the screw. The device is still hand-activated, but some mechanical or other advantage is gained by exploiting a few of the principles of mechanics. In the third kind, the motive power is removed from the user to his instrument or beyond. The domestic animal draws the plough, providing the brute strength to which the farmer gives intelligent direction. Animal power is not yet abandoned; even today the horse is used to set in motion such machines as the cider-press and the hay-elevator. Again, the large forces of nature are employed—wind, streams and ocean currents. The grindstone that was formerly worked by hand is greatly enlarged, set in a building and connected to wind-vanes or water-wheels. Finally, and this is where metals are essential, there is the tool most representative of our time, one which relies upon the combustion of substances placed within it, whether violent and rapid oxidation in the case of gunpowder or petrol, or subdued like that of wood and coal. (The electric dynamo is simply a means of transforming energy, provided by the combustion of oil or coal or by wind and water, into an easily transmissible and convertible form.) Instruments of the fourth kind have not, of course, entirely replaced the others; there remain hand-tools for many kinds of work; wind and water power are still used without conversion; the simplest tools exist side by side with the most advanced, though evolution proceeds fastest among the last comers.

This is the trend of the quondam hand-tool; from the easily tired hand that once held it, it is removed to the almost indefatigable machine. The abilities of the machine are just those which the man lacks. Increasing automatism means increasing accuracy, nor does steel tire like the protoplasmic tissue; because the machine has no mind it does not make mistakes, it is not wayward; there is scarcely a limit set to its magnitude, as there appears to be among living things; its scale is variable from the wrist-watch to the power-station of Dnieprostroy; its strength and subtlety range from the tremor of a needle to millions of horse-power; above all, the machine is a specialist, built for a narrow purpose, so that the whole and each one of its parts are able to perform their functions superlatively well.

As it is improved the machine departs further from the being it serves, though it never quite loses all contact. Increasingly the machine is given the mechanism for its self-direction and self-preservation. By thermostats, fuses, governors, and automatic devices of all kinds, the machine begins to control itself; moreover, though this self-regulation is only in its initial stages, it is more accurate, less temperamental, than the human care. The most advanced machines tend to become ever less dependent upon the human factor; they tend to resemble less mere prolongations of the human body than, superficially, monstrous organisms. But buried in the web of girders and wheels and axles, there are to be found those simple hand-tools which are not so changed but what even a Cro-Magnon might recognize them—the cutters, scrapers and hammers, going about precisely the same business as himself, but how differently!

2. Our second type of tool is for locomotion, a substitute for legs. Everywhere wind and water are in motion, and many animals, as we saw in Chapter II, are so organized as to make good use of these great but intractable natural vehicles. More selective creatures rely upon their bodily energy, produced by the metabolic processes, to shift from place to place. So man commenced, using only legs and arms for moving about. But this admirable self-dependence carries with it limitations of range and velocity, and he reverts, [5] while still preserving some of his own powers, to using the energy of nature. The winged seeds are adapted so that the wind bears them along. Man adapts his instruments, not his body, to make similar uses of circumstance.

The instruments for locomotion have proceeded along much the same lines as those which endow the hand with new powers. As early in human history as the Neolithic Age, dogs, sheep, goats, cattle and pigs appear to have been especially associated with man; horses were domesticated later. At first wild animals must have been tamed; afterwards, perhaps not long after, they were truly domesticated, that is, bred by man. The horse, the ox, the camel and others were eventually made to bear human burdens. Man became for the time being quadrupedal, a kind of little old man of the sea at their expense. Similar behaviour is not unknown among lower animals.

The invention of the wheel was a more important and more typically human performance. It introduced an entirely new device into the world. It is one of the most splendid feats of early man, a

---

5   *Paroles Francaises,* 2nd series. (Eng. Trans., Hibbert Journal, 1915, pp. 473-474.

justification, if one were needed, of Life's enterprise of artifice, an example of the peculiar fertility of this wayward and bastard branch of the evolutionary tree. Men have searched nature for evidences of a wheel and have thought they had found it. But protoplasm is no material for wheel-building; at the hub there is a discontinuity which life abhors. But perhaps it is too much to claim absolute novelty for the wheel. The germ of the idea appears in the insect world, where the Scarabaeus makes his pellets into spheres, so trundling easily what he cannot carry. But the wheel with the axle fixed to it, and later the wheel that rotates about its axle, could not have been imitated from, and were probably not suggested by, anything in nature. Possibly they arose from the logs which are placed under a heavy object so that it may be rolled along.

The wheel and the hand-cart once invented, it remains to harness some domestic animal to the latter, and so make of the two one instrument. From prehistoric times until little more than a century ago, the horse and the horse-drawn vehicle remained the swiftest and most useful means of locomotion over a great part of the world. During that long period evolution was concerned with trappings and unessential details, scarcely progressing at all in the direction of speed. Then the steam-engine, with its greater velocity and endurance, replaced the living motor, and later the petrol engine completed the victory of the efficient dead over the deficient living. In the fight between the automobile and the horse the machine must win. Instead of sitting on the back of an animal that has become specialized for speed among other things, a man crawls inside a device that is specialized for nothing else than convenient locomotion.

He has conquered the sea as he has conquered the land. At best man is but a poor swimmer. Though he sometimes toyed with the idea of harnessing the speedy and strong of the sea, as he did those of the land—the dolphin appears to have been the most popular project—sea-life is intractable material, and he must rely upon his own efforts and the provisions of nature. First the boat is propelled by man-power, aided and impeded by winds and tides; then it is driven before the wind, which, cunningly utilized, is employed to drive vessels even against itself. And finally the invaluable wheel, this time one that wedges and pushes its way through the water, finds its way into the new element, and, driven by steam and oil engines, makes the ship's motion less dependent upon its crew than ever before.

By enveloping himself in a corpus of specialized organs, man has enlarged his habitat till he is become easily the most versatile of creatures, at home on sea or on land, under the sea or in the air. He is now a flying amphibian, and his performance in strange surroundings compares favourably with that of each of the living specialists. The aeroplane out-distances the V-shaped flock of geese; the liner out-rivals even the fabulous among marine monsters; the automobile makes the legs of the swiftest seem like ineffectual flippers. And yet man is almost the same kind of animal as when he first handled a stone, little dreaming of what that pebble would grow into.

3. As the limbs have their appendages and substitutes, so also have the integuments of skin and hair. Gerald Heard puts it eloquently thus: 'As Life kept man from growing his weapons on himself so that he might become not merely a Briareus but *homo ferox,* become at a moment *homo faber,* so it stripped him of his thin pelt and left him

with a wilted fibrous crest (the simians, the nearer they approach to man, lose any pretensions to beauty of coat) that it might crown him with glory and honour and infinite variety.' [6] Man's nakedness as he pushes north and south has to be covered against cold winds and fiery sun, but the new pelt becomes much more than an insulator, it becomes brilliant or sombre, fantastic or gorgeous at will, and instinct with inexhaustible social meanings.

Every kind of organism throws up against the world some sort of covering, hard or soft, prim or gay. The integument may serve as supporting skeleton, defensive armour, insulator and disguise. It may be as effective as a tortoise's or as inconvenient as the hermit crab's whose whelk shell is too small for it. The organism may be more weighted down with defensive armour than any mediaeval knight, or as free from encumbering fortifications as the defenceless but nimble rabbit. Nature gives her heavy suits of mail with one hand and takes her heavier price with the other. She has a certain rough justice.

The persecuted frail creature becomes adapted or perishes. It survives by acquiring lethal weapons, armour, a foul taste and a colour to advertise the fact, an elaborate camouflage, or even a terrible appearance without the power it simulates. It is man's way, and the way of some other creatures, to make himself armour and shelter from convenient bric-a-brac, from borrowed plumes and coats, from vegetable fibre. The caddis-fly larva builds itself a home of small stones or fragments of shell; the hermit crab tucks its tender abdomen into a shell and drags it awkwardly along, borrowing

---

6   *Narcissus*, p. 23

instead of building. Man's fortune was in his head, certainly not in deadly claws or scaly armour. His artificial fighting appendages did away with some of his need for defence against other animals, but cold and heat and hostile men rendered some improvement upon nature's scanty gifts a necessity, at least where conditions were very severe. The origin of clothes, however, is rather to be found in the many objects which were worn as ornaments, and there is no doubt that a sense of modesty arose as the result of raiment. Men did not know that they were naked, become ashamed, and sew themselves aprons, as the story goes, but become ashamed because they were *covered*. The clothes are so much a part of man that he is shocking without them! Nor, apparently, did they find that fairly cold weather demanded some protection. Throughout Papuasia complete nudity is not uncommon, and in spite of the severe climate, the Fuegians wear very little clothing, only a loin-cloth, with a loose skin thrown over the shoulders. [7]

Mr. Gerald Heard has pointed out the roughly common purpose of the arts of building and costume, and drawn an interesting parallel between their respective evolutions. Some of their functions, and particularly their primitive ones coincide. A house may be looked upon as an especially static, roomy and substantial suit of clothes and armour. It takes the place of rain-coat and great-coat and, if fortified, of panoply. No other animal wears a double artificial integument as man does, or a triple one as he used to do in the fortified city. But though many of the functions of clothes and buildings are nearly

---

[7]   *Handbook to the Ethnographical Collections,* Brit.Mus., pp.121 & 302

identical, we cannot trace them to any common ancestor. The first raiment was merely a trophy or a charm, the first home a rock-shelter. And modern developments in domestic building have but served to increase the distinction between costume and architecture. An Englishman's home, so famed as his castle, draw-bridge, moated, circled round with baileys and palisades, is fast become the reverse—a gateway to the life and wealth of the community, a nucleus to which are brought the services which bind the individual to society.

Nevertheless, the house and the clothes remain a kind of artificial skin. The Tasmanian woman who screamed when a certain French officer pulled off his gloves, thought that he was removing his skin. This anecdote has been cited as an illustration of the stupidity of the savage, but beneath the woman's impulse was a deeper reasoning, for the gloves were in fact but a removable skin. Though there is a vast gulf between the ideas which led Bruno to say that his hat was alive when his head was inside it, and those which lead a Pueble Indian to regard the clang of a pot when it breaks as the cry of pain when the spirit departs from the vessel, [8] superstition may conceal some glimmerings of a wisdom that high intelligence overlooks.

The house, itself an instrument, contains many others for supplementing various bodily organs. We seldom realize what we owe to such simple things as chairs and other quadrupedal devices, which give a man the great advantage of a support to his back and as many legs as an insect—though four of them are wooden and immobile, they are none the less legs or useful for that. But we have

---

8   A. C. Haddon, *Evolution in Art*, p. 128

not yet come to such a pass that we, like some of our domestic plants, can no longer support our weight unaided.

4. We lighten the work of our digestive organs as well as of our muscles, passing the raw food through what are really preliminary digestive processes. Victuals are gathered in the field, some of the dross is removed, they are cleaned and prepared, made tender by cooking, and stored ready for use. All the machines and culinary utensils involved in these operations are in the nature of artificial digestive organs, apparatus by which food comes nearer to the finally assimilable product. And the drain, so bowel-like in appearance, is an artificial prolongation of the digestive tract.

5. In certain instances the instrument has begun to penetrate the body. The dentist provides us with false teeth, (artificial certainly, but why *false*?) and the business of the surgeon is to work upon the living tissue with his tools. Some remarkable instruments are used for this purpose, such as those which are introduced, by way of the mouth, into the gullet and air passages for inspection and the removal of foreign bodies, or the Albee bone mill, which is a set of miniature machine tools, enabling the surgeon to work far more rapidly and accurately than by the older methods. These are but temporary accessories; there remain the straps, buckles, crutches, and all the semi-permanent devices of the orthopaedist, artificial larynges and certain other more normal bodily aids, all of which go to show that man is often far from content with his natural body, and that even the healthiest have commenced to make it artificial. Surgery remains negative; will it ever become positive so that a man may tamper with

his body for all kinds of purposes? Beauty specialists have set out in this direction, but their work is insignificant beside that of the races that cicatrize the skin, modify the shape of the head, breasts and feet, or pierce and distend the lips and ears with large stone plugs, and produce all manner of deformations of great interest to the ethnographer, but of no practical advantage.

6. At least as important as the extensions which we have so far described, are the artificial means of amplifying our senses, instruments which reveal the things which eye hath not seen nor ear heard, and so enrich the mind while they prolong the body. The microscope, for example, opened up an entirely new order of things strange and exciting. Man lived in a world with a very limited space-scale; then came an appendage, a few hard lenses added to the adaptable eye lens, and with them a new world, where ugliness is resolved into beauty and seeming coarseness into the finest filigree. His senses are not sharpened by the optical instrument any more than his legs are strengthened by the automobile. He, the bare body, remains essentially as he was, but, so enlarged, he can see the moons of Venus and the intricate pattern of the diatom where before he could see nothing.

An inquisitive animal who wished to discover what the Earth was like, to explore all the lands and seas of the world and the remarkable creatures that live in them, might achieve his object in one of two ways. Having become exceptionally versatile and energetic, inured to every kind of environment in turn, capable of travelling great distances, and almost immortal, he might set out on a world tour of inspection, see, hear, taste all that was to be found, then retire to contemplate, to revive his experiences.

Our hypothetical animal has an alternative course to the same goal—to grow to the size of the earth, to enlarge rather than shift himself, to become a hollow sphere of sense organs and ramified nervous system, a huge and wonderful plant-like creature, dominating all lesser creatures. He would then spare himself the trouble of exposing himself to the hazards of globe-trotting. There would be no need then to move at all; at the most the local adjustment of a sense organ would be all that were needed. Moreover, he would no longer be obliged to rely upon his dim and vanishing memories for all else besides the momentary appearance of a narrow environment. In quick succession he might attend to what his sense organs in places poles apart were presenting to him. His mental content would be enormously enriched. And if, finally, he were able somehow to make matter so preserve the impressions of the past that aspects of the past might be revived at will, then this animal would be god-like, an Earth-Organism with prodigious faculties.

This adventurous creature is of course man, not man as he is, but man as he might become. Strangely enough he is taking both roads at once, the road of travel and the road of growth. Modern communications have made it possible for a few to tour the world, and to many there is the opportunity of adding to the body the means of swift locomotion, so that experience may be gained in various environments in the course of a lifetime. But along the other road we have made a more conspicuous progress, gained greater advantages, and become more civilized. By artificial growth, by addition, not by rushing to and fro, the mind of man has gained new windows in every place, and his sensual apparatus become world-wide.

At its start this second path gives scarcely a clue to the strange places whither it leads. When, by its actions, one member of a herd conveys panic to another, there we see the beginnings of this extra-corporeal growth. As soon as there is communication between animals of the same species, or even of different species, however vague it may be, we have what begins to amount to an extended sense range. In this way a man learns of danger, not by investigating the appearances in person, but by proxy; he employs other organs than his own to perceive, and to produce an appropriate symbol or a re-presentation of the event, a sign that is immediately interpreted by the recipient, expanded by the aid of his imagination into a mental reconstruction of what has occurred, and leads to the suitable actions. A terror-stricken member of an animal herd probably awakens but the dimmest imaginings in the others. But from the human representation (whether it be a partial re-enactment as in gesture, onomatopoeia or graphics, or a mere symbol—a conventional sound or movement or writing, signifying something quite unlike itself), the individual builds up a series of ideas which correspond, to some degree, to what has happened. He is thus enabled, after a sort, to 'see' and 'hear' at a distance, though not clearly; to learn something of far-away places and people without making a journey; in brief, to extend his body by adding human instruments. We are told that travel broadens the mind. It may; but to use travellers as your tools, to read them and talk to them, is a kind of travel that has a greater time-range, and may be even more salutary.

In this chapter we are not concerned with aesthetic representations as such, but with the faithfulness with which an event is reconstructed in the mind of one who uses an external medium to become aware of it. This mental verisimilitude by no means depends for its accuracy upon the appropriateness of the intervening symbol of the skill of the imitator. Thus, though the natural language of imitative sounds and gestures and cries of joy and pain, was an invaluable stepping-stone, it was extremely limited in its application. The more arbitrary sound-symbol has the incalculable advantage of standing for the qualities and values of things, for inimitable and intangible relations, for things unusual and difficult to describe, for subtle meanings and fine distinctions. Paradoxically, it is because words need bear no resemblance to the things they signify, that they are immeasurably more useful and accurate than imitative sounds. They are so because they rely upon the memory and imagination of the person who rebuilds mentally the event for himself, obtaining thus a far more concrete picture than could be otherwise obtained, except, of course, by the experience direct.

While the written and spoken word were being elaborated, and were in turn endowing man with improved mental powers, the art of communication had progressed a long way upon another course which in some respects pointed in the opposite direction. Long before we have any evidence of speech and writing, at such remote periods as the Magdalenian and the Solutrian, men made excellent pictures of animals which are not only tolerable similitudes but works of great vigour and beauty. In the periods that followed, draughtsmanship declined; the subject was analysed and not seen as a whole; preconceived ideas distorted the vision of the artist.

It remained for more civilized men to return to more accurate portrayal. As the painter (I do not speak of him *qua* artist) sets down more faithfully the things he sees, I have less need to fill out the picture with ideas of my own. Roughly, his contribution is inversely proportional to mine. If he draws unskilfully I shall have mentally to correct his picture, straighten some lines and curve others, supply deficiencies and delete the superfluous. Even when the line-drawing is moderately representational I must in my imagination erase the thick boundary line which is never seen in nature, give instead textures to plain surfaces, supply the third dimension and colour and tone, if I wish to see again what the draughtsman has seen. He gives half-picture, half-symbol, leaving a good deal to the imagination. The naturalistic painter gives colour and a suggestion of texture and depth; the sculptor in bas-relief more than hints at the three dimensions of the sculpture in the round. Finally, the painted statue of stone and the wax figures of our exhibition halls arrive at the limits of this line of achievement. Here we have not a symbol but almost the true appearance of the thing, requiring so little of the spectator that he may be persuaded, like the birds that tried to peck at Zeuxis' grapes, that he has before him the 'real' object. And the pavement artist who, it is said, rubbed a red-herring skin on the paving stone before drawing his picture of the fish, tried, without much success perhaps, to go one step further and add to the visual deception an olfactory one.

The art of representation by symbol or by such delusive but cumbersome appearances, progressed hardly at all from the beginnings of civilization until recently, except for such improvements in technique as the invention of printing and the manufacture of paper. It had reached a *cul-de-sac:* the path of future progress lay in another direction. In 1829 Niepce produced an automatically recorded picture on film of bitumen, and by the middle of the century photographs were much as they are now. At first the immense potentialities of this invention were not apparent. In accuracy, of course, the photograph surpasses any man-made picture, and is of far more value to science. But the camera is much more than a convenient tool for making pictures of things as we see them; not only does it enable us to obtain a view of things removed from us in space and time, but it is an organ, an artificial eye constructed upon exactly the same principle as the natural, through which can be seen what the unaided eye can scarcely see or has never seen—the flight of a bullet, 'invisible' stars, the extended tongue of the chameleon, the bubble held for ever in the act of bursting.

The lenses of the telescope and the microscope are additions to the eye lens, adjusting its focal length and so the retinal image. They extend the range of the bodily organ in space, but the space range of the camera is more extensive; further the camera gives a permanent record extending also, so to speak, the time range of the eye. Instead of the human traveller with his often improbable stories, or the draughtsman whose eye and hand are never perfectly co-ordinated, or the venal portrait painter, we have an artificial instrument, more reliable, more speedy, more economical and more sensitive than the human. What point of view shall be adopted, what details omitted and what shown, how the light shall be filtered, are problems which must be solved by the photographer, and with him also lies the work of developing and printing, which may be done in many ways and well or badly. The human element still remains, but it is well in the background.

The photograph but suggested a third dimension until the stereoscope combined two pictures, giving one that had depth. But the water is still frozen, the youths and maidens are still poised as motionless as upon the Grecian Urn, and they have no colours. The cinematograph released them, gave them first a jerky movement more like marionettes than humans, then a smoother motion, and finally rather unconvincing colour. It does not require any great gift of prophecy to foretell that, in spite of the many obstacles that now appear, the moving, coloured, stereoscopic film, with a sound accompaniment, will soon be with us, and will be improved so that the illusion is well-nigh perfect.

We may now tabulate the successive stages of the art of representation.

The contribution of the external stimulus increases ↓

MODES OF PRESENTATION		THE DATA OF THE EXTERNAL STIMULI					
		2 SPACE DIMENSIONS	3rd SPACE DIMENSION	COLOUR	REVIVAL OF THE PAST	TIME FLOW	TIME FLOW (VARIABLE)
OBJECT IMAGINED (constructed from the data of memory without external stimulus)							
SPOKEN DESCRIPTION	⎫ Human Recording						
WRITTEN DESCRIPTION					▓	▓	
HIEROGLYPH		▓			▓		▓
LINE DRAWING		▓					
PAINTING	⎱ Artificial Modes	▓					
SCULPTURE	⎰		▓				
PHOTOGRAPH	⎱ Permanent Records	▓					
COLOUR PHOTOGRAPH		▓		▓			
CINEMATOGRAPH	⎱ Mechanical Recording	▓				▓	
STEREOSCOPIC FILM		▓	▓			▓	
COLOUR FILM			▓	▓		▓	
COLOUR STEREO-FILM	⎰		▓	▓		▓	▓
DIRECT VISION				▓		▓	
Magnified Diminished							

This table, of course, does not show the exact chronological order of the various modes, nor all of these. Its purpose is to indicate more clearly the general tendencies. It will be seen that, ranged between the unaided imagination and the vision direct, there is a series of means by which one may become aware of an appearance, and that these means involve the increasing use of the artificial as their presentations become more complete, as they approach direct vision.

Proceeding from the top to the bottom of the table, the contribution of the mind, filling out what is supplied externally, tends to decrease as the outside representation becomes more and more complete, though memory must always rely eventually upon external factors and even the direct vision needs to be interpreted in the light of experience. The importance of the written description and of those that follow lies in their permanence, which permits the accumulation of a social heritage and makes it possible for us to take lengthy time-journeys. It is only by relegating to the artificial instrument the task of recording images, that we can so enlarge the scope of our experience that it begins to include a great section of the past, racial experiences become our own, time is made to flow fast or slowly, and new worlds are discovered in our midst.

7. The instruments for re-presenting sounds have evolved along lines somewhat similar to those which we have just considered. Until the spoken tale and the musical composition were translated into symbols that inert matter could preserve, a slow and progressive distortion of the original was inevitable. Most of us, however, have not learned to build up mental tunes on the basis of the written score as we have learned to be 'transported' by literature, and very few would be content merely to read music. Between the composer and ourselves there is interposed a human instrument, the performer, who has not yet been replaced by any mechanical device. The gramophone and wireless are not substitutes for this interpreter, they simply extend his range and render many of his brother musicians

unnecessary. It is now possible to draw the track of sound waves, which may be played mechanically. Possibly one day the composer will not need his human interpreters. At the moment it seems that the labour involved in draughting an elaborate composition in this way would preclude the use of wave-writing. But it is not art with which we are concerned here. To obtain information as to any sound that could not be directly experienced, it was formerly necessary to bring the imagination to bear upon noises made by the voice or a musical instrument—a poor make-shift. Now, of course, the gramophone is an efficient extension of the aural apparatus as the film is of the visual.

The mantle of prophecy having fallen upon Mr. Aldous Huxley, we are warned of the 'feelies', amongst other terrors. This chapter of his jeremiad may conceivably be fulfilled, the artificial conveyance of tactual impressions may before long be contrived, and it is just possible, also, that men will attend olfactory concerts in some Queen's Hall of the future. But there are slender grounds for fears or hopes of such things, in the immediate future. Man has far to go—or rather, more to grow—before he can afford to become a static receptor connected to a completely efficient range of sense organs embracing the earth. He must still go abroad to gain experience. Given the sound-colour-stereo-movie, and radio presentations to correspond, given also a great multiplication of artificial eyes and ears in every place, and the ability to choose which of these shall be attended to at any moment, even then, though distance would scarcely exist upon earth, the artificial organs could not convey an impression quite as satisfactory as the experience direct. Add to this the inability to touch, smell and taste most of the things presented, the incapacity to control perfectly the artificial organs, and the poverty of selection this entails, and it is clear that man, the monster Earth-Man, is as yet undeveloped; his artificial evolution is but a thing of yesterday and today. We can dimly perceive his tomorrow, but what of the day after? He may be denuded of all his outgrowths, his life become 'nasty, brutish and short', or his artefacts may flourish and bear wondrous fruit. Who can tell?

From any account, however summary, of our artificial instruments, some mention of the many animals and plants of economic importance cannot be omitted.

The extent to which we have deliberately modified such organisms is the measure of their artificiality. Since we have changed a little most of the creatures in our service, and some of them a great deal, we may justly term these organisms artificial, at least in part. This branch of human endeavour is, of course, nothing else than an elaboration of the symbiotic relationships between organisms, where either of two creatures is the tool of the other.

Beasts of burden have already been mentioned; there remain numerous other uses to which organisms may be put. All the edible fauna of the earth and sea, and the plants whose fruits, leaves, stems and roots find their way onto our tables, are so many factories for building up our food for us, or, if you will, they are so many mouths and gullets of ours, unwittingly toiling without rest in our service, doing for us what we cannot do for ourselves. But though we cannot imitate their methods, we are often able to improve their effectiveness. The wild wheat of Mount Hermon is as different from the domesticated as crab-apples are from Cox's Orange Pippins. The study of Mendelian heredity among the grasses has led to the production of types that are deliberately adapted to the conditions met with in all kinds of places and climates. And everywhere it is one of the most important tasks of the experimental biologist to provide the most efficient apparatus attainable, for building from earth and air nourishing and delectable foods. He is among our more valuable technicians.

Some of our domestic animals are more useful in life than in death. The hen changes household scraps and corn into a delicacy that no chemist can contrive, and we have perverted the natural use of the cow. Hens and cows are cheaper, more sensible (machines do not find their way home from pasture,) and on the whole less trouble than the machine which the chemist would contrive, if he could, for turning out eggs and milk. For less serious purposes, we can produce such monsters as dachshunds and bulldogs and pouter pigeons; and all sorts of scientifically useful tricks can be played with lower animals—grafting the front half of a grog's embryo onto the hind half of the embryo of another species of frog, so that a composite creature is produced, or performing an operation on a toad so that it grows to maturity with no fewer than six hind legs.

No less interesting are the uses that men have made of the sense organs of animals. The natives of the Torres Straits tie their fishing line to the tail of a sucker-fish, which finds and attaches itself to a turtle, thus guiding the fisherman. In India and the East generally, the art of falconry is still practised; the carrier pigeon finds its way where the aviator, in spite of maps and instruments, may lose his; and we have contrived to use the superior faculties of bloodhounds, retrievers, St. Bernards, and a host of other creatures, as supplements to our own lacking endowment.

And so the story proceeds. Man is not likely to rest content till every creature from which he can exact some service has been added to his body, and all the rest have been exterminated, made the subjects of endless experiment, or preserved where he may occasionally view the living forms that he has so completely outstripped in the race for dominion.

Observe how often he reverts to the ways of lower creatures.

The main shapes arise!

Shapes of Democracy total, result of centuries,

Shapes ever projecting other shapes,

Shapes of turbulent manly cities,

Shapes of the friends and home — givers of the whole earth,

Shapes bracing the whole earth and braced with the whole earth.

Walt Whitman, Song of the Broad Axe

CHAPTER V

The Instruments of Society

All men are social and all their tools are social products. Only in an enduring community could artefacts accumulate improvements while generations pass. Every tool has a long history interwoven with the history of races and cultures. It is of a piece with man. In every detail of its present form and employment there could be traced, if we had the eye to see them, the strivings and triumphs of myriads of men and the traditions of a hundred cultures. No idea so foreign to the nature of the thing of use, no influence so removed from its operations, but may be brought to bear upon it and leave their mark. The everyday utensil, like the creature it belongs to, has its roots deep in the race's past.

In another sense tools are social. In the previous chapter we described the extensions of the individual as though they were his and his alone. This is an abstracted view which must be offset by a consideration of the tool's place in society, where one instrument often serves many men, and extensions are held in common. Though social relations are first and foremost psychical, there are also physical bases to these, namely, the natural and artificial bodies of men. Beyond a certain point artificial organs become social. A man's house and garden, for example, may be his own, for his sole use, but the cables and pipes, the roads and rails, which bind his home to other homes and to centres of distribution are organs of the community. The natural bodies of men are distinct; their artificial bodies are woven into a great mass. And it is this common tissue of fabricated material that is fast binding men into one physical whole, the organic foundations of what Graham Wallas has called the Great Society.

We have now before us the material for making a sketch of the 'well-developed' man of our day. Unlike the painting that includes, besides the body proper, only the sitter's clothes and his chair, our portrait would embrace all that is interposed between his naked body and nature, all the bulwarks thrown up by artifice against the onslaughts of crude and undisciplined circumstance. No frame of ours could contain the completed picture, no canvas compass all the ramifications of our subject. It would be necessary to terminate every line at an arbitrary point, to vignette the margins. For almost at once the individual's extensions become those of other men also, and his greater body is society's; and who shall say where the social instrument ends and raw nature begins? Is the dammed and deepened river that drives the dynamo an organ of the community no less than the power station? And if it is so, shall the spring that feeds the stream, the rain that waters the earth, the clouds and the ocean and the sun itself, be called the instruments of man?

These are the blurred edges. At the centre of the picture is the clear focal point, the living tissue. Its first need is food. A few thousand years ago a man's fathers had to leave their shelters to search for what they could find. Now he is urban and well-to-do. His cave, though still cavelike, has become changed in appearance, but far more in use. To this outer integument, within which he moves freely, are attached the channels through which his food, drink, clothes and much else, are brought to him. If we suppose our subject to live in a well appointed service flat, he has there around himself the terminal points of a series of organs, to each of which he may apply his body in turn; he is a body moving within the tiny cell of a greater one. If he would eat, there is a service lift communicating with the kitchen of the building. Roads with their police, vehicles with their drivers, telephones with their operators, link the kitchen with the public shops and stores; and these are supplied by the factories and mills and warehouses which are the organs of millions. It is not till we arrive at the reaper-and-binder at work in the cornfields of Canada and Russia, the net drawn through the water by the steam trawler, the mechanical potato digger crawling across the land, the river diverted into the impounding reservoir, that we discover the organs which first engulf the raw foodstuffs. These are the great communal mouths, artificial limbs and maws which hunt down and gather and drink copiously the nourishment of society. Between these insatiable jaws and the man in the flat is arranged a system of organs which yield the food to him at last, half digested already and often altered beyond recognition. His fleshly body merely continues the process by other means, building up the body-food into the cell-food, as the social organs have built the social-food out of nature's provision and the kitchens below have made social-food into body-food. And the drain, for a short distance his own, soon becomes social property, the city's sewer, and ends at the disposal farm—a communal excretory system. The exterior body, responsible for converting and preparing his comestibles, carries away the residue and so completes its work on behalf of the living body at the centre.

So considered, modern man is a creature unrivalled in legend or the imagination. The world is his kitchen garden and game preserve, and it is his home. Social organs make it possible to hear the stir of the wind in antipodean trees, the faintest bird's note in American forests, and the whisper of a man wherever he may be—and all this we mostly take for granted! Other organs send his own voice to the ends of the earth, enable him to see at a thousand leagues' range, and to set matter in motion far and wide. Corresponding to every service he enjoys and every power he wields, there is a social organ, comprising machines and implements and men, which serves him. Born into a society, a man finds himself in the midst of systems of such organs, ready to be linked to his puny body of flesh, upon the understanding, as a rule, that he also shall serve when the time comes.

Such considerations as these, and a number of others, have led many to describe a society as an 'organism'. The analogy between communities and living creatures is taken for granted when we speak of the *heart* of the city, *arterial* roads, the *head* of the State. Almost as soon as men began to think seriously about social organization they noted that the social body bore curious resemblances to the human. Plato, in the *Republic,* compares the officers of the State to the impulses of the citizen, making counsellors, auxiliaries and traders in the former, correspond respectively to reason, passion and desire in the latter—a factitious and unconvincing parallel. St. Paul sees the members of the Church as the organs of a mystical Body. Shakespeare's Menenius tells the parable of the good belly, which says to the insubordinate members of the body:-

"True it is my incorporate friends,...

That I receive the general food at first

Which you do live upon; and fit it is,

Because I am the storehouse and shop

Of the whole body: but, if you remember,

I send it through the rivers of your blood,

Even to the court, the heart,—to the seat o' the brain;

And, through the cranks and offices of man,

The strongest nerves and small inferior veins

From me receive that natural competency

Whereby they live:"

And Menenius explains to his audience:

"The senators of Rome are this good belly,

And you the mutinous members."

But this is poetic metaphor. To many mystics the human race, or some portion of it, appears in the likeness of a man. Swedenborg, for example, has many passages much as this:—

"Every man is from infancy introduced into that divine Man whose soul and life is the Lord, and in that divine Man and not apart therefrom, he is led and taught from His divine Love according to His divine Wisdom. But as man is never deprived of his freedom, he can only be led and taught in the degree that he receives the Lord as if by the exercise of his own power. Those who receive the Lord are led to their own places by infinite windings like those of a meandering stream, almost as the chyle is carried through the mesentery and the lacteal vessels into the receptacle and from this through the thoracic duct into the blood, and so to its destination. Those who are not receptive are separated from those who are within the divine Man, just as the faeces and urine are separated from man. These are arcana of angelic wisdom which man can in some measure understand; but there are many more which he cannot." *Divine Providence,* 164,V,6.

And Blake, possibly influenced by his reading of Swedenborg, wrote:—

"Mutual in one another's wrath all renewing,

We live as One Man: for, contracting our Infinite senses,

We behold multitude; or expanding, we behold as One,

As One Man all the Universal Family."

Jerusalem, f.38, 11. 16-19

Hobbes, in the *Leviathan,* has a peculiar version of the organismic 'theory', in which he likens the State to 'an artificial man; though of greater stature and strength than the natural.' Auguste Comte made some use of the doctrine, but the first philosophers to give it something like the appearance of a full-fledged theory were Herbert Spencer and Schäffle. In his *Principles of Sociology,* Spencer was at great pains to show the many similarities, both in constitution and development, between organisms and what he calls super-organisms, or societies. After many pages devoted to these analogies, he concludes by saying 'This comparison has been justified to a degree that could scarcely have been anticipated.' And of another kind of society Bergson has said:' When we see the bees of a hive forming a system so strictly organized that no individual can live apart from the others beyond a certain time, even though furnished with food and shelter, how can we help recognizing that the hive is really, and not metaphorically, a single organism, of which each bee is a cell united to the others by invisible bonds. [1]

Other thinkers, approaching the problem of the nature of a society from the psychological side, have attributed to the community a 'group mind' and sometimes even a 'corporate consciousness'. Prof. McDougall, though repudiating the latter conception, has made out a case for the former. 'We may fairly define a mind' he says, 'as an organized system of mental or purposive forces; and, in the sense so defined every highly organized human society may properly be said to possess a collective mind.' [2] For Hegel the State was a mystical being, a kind of god to whom its citizens owed unquestioning obedience. In their interpretation of the relations between the individual and society, the English idealists Green and Bosanquet have adopted, though in a modified form, the Hegelian metaphysical theory of the State. [3] The French sociologist Espinas speaks of a collective consciousness, *une fusion de consciences multiples en une seule;* and Durkheim considered a society to have a mental life of its

1   *Creative Evolution,* p.175
2   *The Group Mind,* p.9
3   See Bosanquet's *Philosophical Theory of the State,* and L.T. Hobhouse, *Metaphysical Theory of the State,* for a criticism.

own made up of 'collective representations' which are to some extent independent of 'individual representations'.

The organismic and the group mind theories of community have been attacked frequently and with some asperity. Their opponents have pointed out that the organism has a unity which is in no instance to be found in a society. The life of the individual is not lost in the life of a community in a way that is at all comparable with the subordination of cells and organs to the wellbeing of the organism as a whole. The purpose of the individual is often at variance with what most consider to be the general good, and it is (they say) exceedingly difficult to speak of the cells and organs of an organism as having purposes of their own. And these objections are re-enforced by stressing what are, after all, very obvious differences; the discontinuity of the units of a society and their mobility stand in clear contrast to the cohesion of the parts of the organism; societies do not originate, nor live, nor die like organisms; social organs overlap, are inextricably involved in a manner totally unlike the parts of the living creature. Further, the mind of a community, the will of a community, the feelings of a community, though they are more than those of the individual, do not lie within some god-like social mind which is outside men's minds, but they exist only within the minds of the many co-operating individuals that comprise the social unit. Society, says Prof. Maciver, is in each of us.

The large crop of 'refutations' of the organismic theory that followed the Great War was partly due to the view that the deification of the State, and its corollary, the subordination of the citizen to the supposed claims of this being, was either a cause or a symptom of the kind of imperialism which led to that tragic event. But in their endeavour to uphold the claims of the individual and preserve the democratic ideal, some tended to go too far in the opposite direction. On the one hand they were apt to over-estimate the unity of the living organism, in its psychological as well as in its organic aspect, and on the other hand to underrate the dependence of the individual upon the society to which he belongs.

An intermediate view, avoiding both the abstracted individualism of the more mechanical theories and the classification of societies as just one more order of organisms, allows a community of men or of social insects to be a unit, a whole founded upon the co-operation of diverse parts, but *a whole of a different order,* a *new* synthesis with laws of its own, laws which bear no small resemblance to those which govern its parts, but which we must not expect to be reflected in their entirety at any other level. Society is an emergent novelty, the characteristics of which are no more to be adduced from an examination of an isolated member of the society than the behaviour of water may be foretold by examining atoms of hydrogen and oxygen apart from their relations within the molecule.

The theory of emergents, foreshadowed by John Stuart Mill, has been developed by a number of recent and contemporary philosophers under such designations as the Emergent Evolution of C. Lloyd Morgan, the Emergent Vitalism of C. D. Broad, the Epigenesis of James Ward, the Holism of General Smuts, and a few other titles, each of which represents a somewhat different approach from the others, though the broad principles remain the same. Some take for their basic units 'atomic' events, and with others the space-time continuum is a primitive datum. Upon the given foundations, whatever they may be, is reared an ascending hierarchy of wholes, such as electrons, atoms, molecules, complex organic compounds, single cells and multicellular organisms respectively, each of which is an 'organic unity' founded upon relations between wholes belonging to a previous level. Wherever units are mutually dependent, are related to one another so that each is maintained by its relations with the rest, a new and higher whole, with new characters, emerges, and this new whole may itself become related to other wholes of its own level in such a way that a yet higher whole, again with unique characters, emerges. So it may be said that at a certain level materiality has emerged, at a higher level life has arisen, and finally mind has appeared—the crowning emergent of the whole process.

We have already noticed that single cells are frequently integrated, thus forming multicellular organisms. Where there is little differentiation between the component cells, we have a colony which may scarcely be regarded as a true individual, but where different sets of cells take on special functions and division of labour occurs among them, a new unit, whose behaviour is in some respects unique, has arisen out of their mutual dependence.

Having, by the theory of emergents, done something to bridge the gulf between the inert and the living, and between the lowest forms of life and ourselves, some thinkers have been content to push the theory no further. Others, however, have found in societies yet another level of the hierarchy of wholes and parts. Professor W. M. Wheeler has adopted the Spencerian term super-organism for societies, and, while admitting the character of integration at this level to be loose and primitive, says: 'Social aggregates—if we may employ the term 'social' in its broadest sense—may be divided into two great groups, the heterogeneous and the homogeneous, the former comprising the associations of organisms belonging to different species, the latter of individuals of the same species and therefore of common genetic origin. In either group the simplest association obviously obtains between two interacting individuals, the combined behaviour of which may be said to form an emergent pattern different from, though depending on, the functional peculiarities of the two component organisms.' [4] If this be so, it is indeed, as Lloyd Morgan has said, 'beyond the will of man to number the instances of emergence', and there can scarcely be a plant or an animal which is not a part of some such pattern.

Among homogeneous societies, the human is a mere episode of the moment by comparison with those of the social insects. A study of the remains of ants in Baltic amber has led entomologists to the conclusion that ant societies were, in the Lower Oligocene period, much as they are now, differentiated into the same castes and with 'guests' very similar to those of the present day. Man is no pioneer in this field, and in a number of ways his societies are less perfect than the harmonious and ancient communities of bees, wasps, ants and termites.

---

4   *Emergent Evolution and the Social*, pp. 20 & 21

The successive stages in the evolution of insect social organization are well represented by forms now living. The first traces of the tendency appear when the parent lives for some time after egg-laying, and displays some solicitude for the well-being of its family. Thus the earwig, having deposited its eggs in an excavation, rests over them until they hatch, and the male and female dung beetle mount guard over the nest where their larvae are feeding. Here we see the beginnings of a division of labour. The social wasps have gone further. A single fertilized queen founds a nest, laying eggs which develop into three kinds of adults, namely, other queens, which are comparatively large, a few males, and a greater number of workers, which are smaller and generally sterile. The work of the community is shared among its members; the queen's business is to lay eggs, while the sterile workers tend her and her brood.

Though a flourishing hive of social bees may contain as many as 80,000 members, these consist, like the wasp community, of no more than three castes. The vast majority of the bees are workers. The drones, or males, are larger than these, and the queen has a longer abdomen and hyper-developed generative organs. She is in fact simply an egg producing machine, with an output of perhaps a million eggs in her lifetime and a body that is accordingly differentiated from the others—she has upon her legs, for instance, no apparatus for collecting pollen such as the workers possess.

Ant societies have, besides the winged males and females, a worker caste of sterile females which are differentiated into a larger kind, or 'soldiers', and a minor kind, while in certain species there are also types intermediate between these. If we also include within the ant society, as we have every reason to do, their guests, then we have here a considerable diversity of structure and function among its members. These distinctions are even more marked among the termite communities, where from the eggs of one queen are produced several castes, varying in size and form according to their respective duties. First there are the normal winged kings and queens, next a caste very similar to these but with smaller eyes, a smaller brain and less developed sexual organs, and a wingless caste with these organs still smaller. All these are potentially fertile. The fourth kind is a sterile worker with rudimentary eyes or none and a smaller brain, and the fifth is a 'soldier', resembling the last but with much larger eyes and more powerful mandibles.

The success of insect societies is shown by their wide diffusion and great numbers. Evidently this expedient of co-operation has advantages which make for the survival of those organisms which abandon the free-lance life for the communal. The specialization of members as fighters, food getters and reproductive forms, no doubt endows the society with an elasticity that is favourable in combating circumstance. However such differences have arisen between members of one family, it is clear that we have in the ant or termite society a new kind of whole. There is a strict division of labour, accompanied by morphological distinctions and co-operation of the most thorough kind. The pattern of the whole pervades the behaviour of its parts; the actions of each member are capable of interpretation only as we view its relations with the other members; the parts are members of one another and of the whole.

One of the most important differences between an insect society and a human one is that the former consists only of one family, the latter of many families. The result is that, on the one hand, every time a fertilized queen founds a nest, a new society, based upon no other traditions than the instincts of her offspring, and having no material legacy from a previous generation, is established afresh, and eventually perishes with the dissolution or destruction of the family, while, on the other hand, human societies long outlive their members, and owe most of their tendency towards increasing complexity to the fact that material and mental achievements are bequeathed to future generations by many agencies.

Insect societies have been described as more perfect examples of social organization than the human, particularly on account of their more harmonious internal economy and the fact that while amongst men there is little difference between the members of the community, the social insects have castes whose members are organically specialized for their several functions. In our own communities the thinker, perhaps unfortunately for his thinking, has essentially the same skeletal and muscular outfit as the navvy; all men, excepting an insignificant number, are fertile, though some are demonstrably more fitted for propagation than others; the surgeon and the musician have nearly the same fingers as the prize-fighter. But the thinker is no thinker without access to books and other men of his kind; the navvy is no navvy unless he is furnished with the tools that give him that status; the surgeon and the musician have no existence as such until their hands grasp the instruments which alone enable them to fulfil their proper tasks, to become specialized parts of the community. It is the role of the tool to make men into specialists, and without specialization society cannot exist.

As a matter of fact, then, there is a division of labour within a human society which far surpasses that of the ant's nest or the termitarium, and it is founded, not upon the polymorphism of men, but of their instruments. And this division of labour involves mutual dependence, a complex social organisation, and a tendency for the parts of society to constitute together a higher whole which influences profoundly their behaviour. While society, in one of its aspects, is a system of relations between minds, it has a material or organic aspect also, a corpus. Within this material whole must be included as an integral part of it, besides the bodies of men, all the artificial appendages, which, as we have seen, both unite men's extended bodies in one continuous system and permit those bodies to become specialized organs of the community. Tools are as truly part of society, regarded in this way, as men are. Human societies, therefore, though in one sense homogeneous, are heterogeneous also, and embrace domestic animals, domestic plants, machines, means of communication, tools, books, spoken words, and the whole world of artifice. These material things are the indispensable foundations of the society's mental life as it now exists, just as much as the component cells of an animal's body are the material basis for its existence as a mind. Modify in any way the organic groundwork of either the creature or the community, and its mental life is thereby altered, and conversely, mental changes are bound to affect, however slightly, the material body. As mental relations in all their complexity are the invisible bonds which bind men into communities, so the artificial, which is the visible or audible counterpart of these relations, is the cement of the social edifice, the integrative medium that is both built up by and makes possible psychical relations as we know them.

Fabrication is the practice of constructing the organs of the community. Working, as he thinks, for himself and other men, a man unwittingly serves the new whole. The enthusiasm of the inventor, his zeal for construction, the intense satisfaction that comes of successful creative endeavour—these are not apart from the trend of things, but heirs or agents of a universal urge. The builder of houses and railroads is going about essentially the same business as the cell within the body, as the atom within the molecule, as the electron within the atom. He is fulfilling his duties towards his kind, maintaining relations at one level which give rise to a whole at a higher level. It is true that man only is more or less clearly conscious of what he is doing for others, and sometimes dimly aware that he subserves an entity of a higher order than himself. The cell in his body has no thought for him when it performs its characteristic functions; it behaves as it is its nature to do; there are no altruistic motives and no consideration for the emergent pattern. Amongst ourselves also, even when a man has strong humanitarian sentiments, it is himself and others like him that are considered ends, rather than any superhuman individuals, though, of course, the patriot sometimes personifies his country.

But, for all his indispensable preoccupation with himself, man still labours unremittingly on behalf of social wholes. Those who say, quite correctly no doubt, that there can be no worthy end for us but our own fortunes as men, and that States and societies should be as nothing to us except in so far as they exist for the benefit of individual citizens, are apt to assume the possibility of a real antithesis between our well-being and the progressive evolution of communities. It is at least debatable whether there can be any such antithesis; it remains to be demonstrated that Life is so divided against itself. In any case, whether we profess loyalty to Life, to our species, or to community as an individual of a higher grade than ourselves, we are inevitably, even in the profession, acting within such a higher whole and as part of it. It is here in our very midst, pervading every thought and action.

At this pinnacle of the structure of wholes and parts we confront difficulties that are almost as formidable as those which we have to encounter at the base. The electron describing its orbit within the atom is a product of the speculative imagination, and 'super-organisms' are discovered only by an imaginative effort which enables us to withdraw ourselves from society and observe it from outside. We are situated, as it were, so near to the apex that we cannot perceive it clearly, and so far from the foundations that they are shrouded in obscurity. The vista left open to our view lies between these extremes, and only a section of it is well within range, can be focussed clearly. We have an overwhelming mass of 'inside information' concerning the social organism; we have a distinct view of its parts, but these are abstracted; the concrete whole it is difficult to perceive. In analysis we must needs tear apart, and so lose sight of the emergent qualities which spring from togetherness.

But it is not beyond the power of the imagination to overcome to some degree these difficulties. By use of this faculty we can mentally absent ourselves from society, become so enlarged that the Earth appears no bigger than an Amoeba under the microscope, and temporarily put out of mind some of our preconceived ideas upon the subject. Then the Great Society appears, not as a system of mental relations, nor as a mere aggregate of two kinds of things— the one living and the other dead, but as a living metabolic whole comprising units of many kinds. The seeming absurdity of Bruno's statement that his boots and his hat were alive when he wore them, has a core of truth. Certainly they have no life of their own, but neither can certain mineral parts of the animal body be said to have life of their own; like Bruno's boots these parts are caught up within the organic constitution of a whole that lives. A thorough analysis of the protoplasm itself could only reveal at last 'dead' particles. What we know as life in its most primitive form, emerges when relations of a particular kind occur between inert units. More advanced living wholes have incorporated lower living units and, laterally, 'dead' or artificial units also. While we cannot go so far as to say of temples that 'the conscious stone to beauty grew', when we have allowed for the poetic license, Emerson's words are not greatly at variance with the sober fact:-

"Know'st thou what wove yon woodbird's nest

Of leaves, and feathers from her breast?

Or how the fish outbuilt her shell,

Painting with morn each annual cell?

Or how the sacred pine-tree adds

To her old leaves new myriads?

Such and so grew these holy piles,

While love and terror laid the tiles

Earth proudly wears the Parthenon

As the best gem upon her zone."

The influence which the artificial exerts upon social relations can scarcely be exaggerated. If men have made tools, tools also have made men. Though there are many intimate mental and physical relations which do not rest directly upon any such basis, those most characteristic of our age are dependent at every turn upon men's material works and advance *pari passu* with them. One obscure inventor, working at a problem without thought, possibly, of consequences, arrives at last at his solution—an insignificant enough piece of matter, and the shock is felt in the remotest of human habitations. The upshot is incommensurable with the initial movement. A few shapes cut out of a wooden block, and the treasures of learning are no longer the property of a handful but penetrate to the nethermost stratum, transforming utterly the private worlds of innumerable individuals. A drum of water, a fire of coals, and a few pipes cunningly contrived in a forgotten workshop, and many men are not only, like Socrates, citizens of the world in mind, but Earth citizens in fact. A few wires, a little glass and metal subtly organized, and presently the most isolated hamlet, the ship in mid-ocean and the lone flyer, no longer stand apart from the day to day life of the Great Society but are drawn into it by impalpable bonds.

Such are the artificial links that are helping to make of nations a world community and breaking down here and there territorial barriers and barriers of race and colour. But we are observing a tendency and no fully realized fact. The most thoroughly organized society is as yet full of contention and disharmonies. Social integrates of whatever order, whether families, townships, nations or federations of nations, are, for all their complexity, lacking in such unity as the organism has. They intermingle so that none presents an appearance of external wholeness, and each is rent by internal rivalries which war against even the semblance of unity within. On the one hand, national and international organizations override the limits of city and of State, while on the other hand individuals and institutions with conflicting aims tend to divide the community against itself. Such detailed analogies as may exist between the organic foundations of society and those of organisms are irrelevant when this nexus of mental relations is under consideration. If we may speak of communities as individuals at all, their individualities are assuredly of a very low order, and incomparable with men's.

Many set-backs, many misunderstandings and international calamities, hinder the welding of States into a greater Federation, and, though wars and rumours of wars do not frequently rend the nation from within, there is no lack of strife, which is none the less real for being bloodless, none the less severe for all the fine phrases which gloss it over. In spite of that harmonious co-operation which is the very groundwork of society, competition and struggle are only partially alleviated, and it is no doubt desirable that some of this friction, at least in certain of its aspects and in modified form, should remain. Even in the smooth working of the animal body, the struggle for food between various tissues continues, and if by any chance the supply wanes, one kind of tissue will succeed better than another until its relative bulk will be far in excess of its more impoverished competitors. [5] What happens in societies is very similar, though men do not prey upon one another's living bodies, but upon the artificial extensions of these. Extra-corporeal organs are at once the spoils of victory and the weapons in the conflict, and they grow as they become more effectual. The race is not to the swift of limb, nor the battle to the strong of arm: the prize goes to the artificially well-developed. Fortunately, competition is not at all points inconsistent with mutual aid, and in fending for himself a man often, perhaps usually, assists others; even he may bear the welfare of others in mind no less than his own, but such a man is an exception. As a rule the benefit of the community is not the individual's conscious aim. His aim is rather growth, the artificial extension of Butler's 'well-developed' man; and though such expansion often involves that of others also and the furtherance of social unity, it is in other instances definitely antisocial development at others' expense and at the cost of a partial disintegration of society. And if to some of these social diseases the medicine of the law may be administered with good effect, there remain many ailments which too often pass for normal health or for eternal and irremediable disabilities.

5   W. Roux, *Der Kampf der Teile im Organismes.*

We will take a few examples by way of illustration. Thirty years ago, saddlers, blacksmiths and coachbuilders were numerous and prosperous craftsmen, making with simple tools the various devices associated with the horse and the horse-drawn vehicle. By diligently plying their trade these men were able to add to themselves a certain number of artificial organs, the conveniences of private life. Doubtless many of them took no small degree of interest in their craft, and looked upon themselves occasionally as very useful members of society, but perhaps to a greater degree they were concerned with the accumulation of property and with the comforts and prestige that come of artificial growth. Meanwhile, other groups of men were working with other tools upon other materials, though with the same end of personal growth in view. These were the makers and inventors of automobiles, who used their tools and mental faculties to such good effect that they were able to produce an instrument that proved for them an immense advantage in the struggle for artificial growth, and for others a valuable specialized extension. The car was, for its makers not so much an appendage for locomotion as a weapon calculated to prevail against the weapons of other groups and, in particular, against the weapons of those concerned with the horse-drawn vehicle. Not by reason of their general harmfulness but because of their usefulness to the community, the more modern weapons enriched and extended the machine builders while they disarmed most of the craftsmen of the older group, impoverishing them as a class. Here, though a small number suffer in the struggle, there is a material gain for the community. Elsewhere in the field society's gain is less considerable. Each of a dozen shopkeepers in a small town, offering for sale similar commodities, uses every legitimate means in his power to snatch as many patrons from the others as he is able, not surely because he is convinced that his wares are superior in any way, but in order to grow artificially at the expense of his competitors. The amount of wealth which is likely to be accumulated by these tradesmen collectively cannot vary within very wide limits. Accordingly, the relative success of one involves the relative failure of the rest. It is, of course, probable that competition here assists somewhat in the maintenance of efficient service, and that the many derive a slight benefit while the few are injured seriously. But there is no lack of intermediate stages between the tradesman and the *entrepreneur* within the law and the thief outside the law; these all have for their aim the accumulation of artificial organs by processes that benefit few or none besides themselves. Their tactics of warfare are somewhat different, but the spoil is, in part at least, essentially similar to what the most respectable of social benefactors desires to secure by all the approved means in his power.

The immeasurably complex relations between all forms of life, corresponding in part to what is called the struggle for existence, are the means by which life as a whole is self-regulated, by which progress to higher forms is made possible and a certain balance is maintained. When a number of individuals stand in intimate and reciprocating relation to one another, when, in other words, a higher individual is constituted, though the actions of the parts are determined by their effects upon the whole, still there is struggle between them. If we can scarcely say that cells and tissues have motives, at least each kind has its characteristic behaviour. In this direction it 'strives', and the outcome of many such divergent strivings is mutual aid and a more or less ordered whole. But when, through causes of which we have all too little knowledge, the regulating factors within the body fail to control the growth of tissue, then we find diseases like cancer, which is due to an abnormal multiplication of cells. The too great success of one part upsets the balance of the whole and disintegration follows.

In society also there must be a delicate adjustment between various human activities. But in many ways the situation is radically changed. We have already noted how man has avoided the polymorphism of the cell in the animal body and even that of the termite, by the employment of detachable organs, so that he is able during one part of his life to follow a narrow expert calling, and for the rest of his time to lead as general and human an existence as he pleases. The elasticity of his mind and the temporary nature of his tools, are his saviours. Unlike the ant or the single cell, he is not born with the capacity to use the instruments belonging to one profession, but with a mind capable of learning the performance of many actions. During the working day he serves the community, carries out the particular work for which he is equipped with the appropriate organs. These he throws aside as soon as work is over. Then he ceases to be a differentiated unit existing for society, a mere cog in the machine, and becomes an end for which the machine is working. It is his dual role to alternate between the condition of an organ of society and that of an individual whose organ is the community as a whole, to be end and means in turn. Those who stress one of these aspects of his life at the expense of the other, incline to overlook the fact that one of the greatest of human discoveries is how to effect a compromise between specialization and generalization, how to enjoy the advantages of belonging to a great community while avoiding to a very great extent the fate that has overtaken so many animal specialists.

Society is founded upon division of labour. It is not beyond the bounds of possibility, however, that a form of social organization which is capable of making use of machines to increase vastly the wealth, and reduce considerably the number of working hours, of the majority, (instead of, as now, inflicting unemployment upon some and long hours of dull labour upon others) will eventually be brought about. In that case, society—using that term to include all its tools— would, as machines were improved, become more and more an organ of the individual and less and less a hard taskmaster. The important problem, so urgent even now, would then be to provide man with such an education as would encourage him to make the best and fullest possible use of the vast organization at his disposal. Spite of all our social maladjustments, machines have already released many from the bondage of utter subordination to the general interests and made possible for some a life where the community exists for the individual, as a vast extension of his body on the one hand, and, on the other, what is of greater importance, an incomparable instrument for obtaining knowledge of the world's past and present.

A man is born with two heritages. In the first place, he is endowed with a certain physical and mental structure capable of development within very wide limits. Further, he inherits a peculiar environment in which these potentialities may be fully realized. It is the play of these two ever interacting worlds, holding the possibility of an infinite number of adjustments, which makes a man what he is. The first part of his inheritance comprises a bodily structure and certain instincts affecting the organism as a whole; the second part includes the social traditions, in particular, all the permanent and semi-permanent works of man, and all the customary relations between man and man, and between man and things. In short, the accumulated experience of the race is made available in the present. The untold wealth of the racial mind and the material objects in which this mind is conserved and expressed, are all at hand to enrich and modify at every turn the life of him who is born amongst them. We live neither to ourselves nor by ourselves. The experience of humanity is our own, and we contribute to it in turn. Somewhat as the developing embryo recapitulates in a few weeks and months the age-long history of its ancestors, as its history is a distorted and hurried reflection of theirs, so the growing child learns the bodily actions of his species, the use of tools and language and writing, and arrives at last at manhood, when his brief struggle has made the results of the long struggle of humanity his own. He has grown to the full stature of man, no mere three or four cubic feet of unstable flesh, but in body a gigantic structure that his fathers have built, and in mind a system of presentations derived, in a great measure, from the minds of innumerable members of his species. In him, and in others like him, the past and its denizens attain a kind of immortality.

Tradition, or the social heritage, is preserved by many agents. It has many vehicles and many aspects. Institutions which outlast the life of generations and even the deaths of empires, unrecorded ways of life which are conveyed to successive generations by precept and example, legends and oral laws—these are some of the modes by which past experience may be brought to bear upon present life. But the message is mutable; in process of time, institutions, myths, customs and unrecorded wisdom are subject to change. The past, though never lost, is scattered and disorganized; its sharp outlines are worn away; it exists only as an ever more diffused and ever less effectual influence in the present. For the artificial is needed to give to the past a permanence which will secure its survival in a purer form, in a condition that renders it a force of value to reason in the regulation of present action.

The power of learning by experience is possessed, according to Professor H. S. Jennings [6], by organisms as primitive as some of the Protozoa, and may perhaps be characteristic of all living things. At its lowest level, the repetition of certain stimuli provokes 'a readier resolution of certain physiological states.' The creature's past is operative in its present. To the heritage it received from the parent cell it has added capital of its own. Higher organisms set out in life with a more substantial endowment, with parental provisioning in the form of the egg-yolk, or they are fed, cared for, and taught the business of life by the parent. In addition, their own physical faculties are more variable, and the beginnings of intelligence enable

---

6   *Behaviour of the Lower Organisms.*

them to learn more and better from their own past experience. The faculty of communication by means of inarticulate sounds and bodily movements, and finally the invention of speech, provided far more efficient means for bringing the experience of many others to bear upon individual behaviour. Moreover, with speech came the capacity to generalize or form concepts, which involved the comparison of the present with the past and made possible the foretelling of the future. In evolution there can be traced, in fact, an increasing tendency for the organism to make greater use of its own past and of the past of an ever growing number of other creatures, belonging to other places and to other times.

Man above all has carried forward this process. After speech, conceptual thought and reason had improved the intrinsic qualities of the unit, by far the most important development took place along other lines—the improvement of communication between the units. There is little or no evidence for any advance in mental capacity during the past three thousand years. Progress, if we may use the term, has been due to very different causes, most of all to the invention of new modes of impressing individual human achievement upon matter, the making of permanent records by artifice, so that each new thinker and constructor builds upon the foundations laid down by his predecessors. It is no longer necessary nor desirable for each generation to build *de novo*, to waste overmuch energy and time in the performance of costly experiments which their forefathers have already made. Though from time to time there must be much revision of plans and an overhauling of subsidiary structures, constructive work is made far easier for the later comers.

The mistakes of our forbears are no less valuable building material for us today than their successes, and the structure of our knowledge is compact of both. And it is precisely the quality which, among others, differentiates the dead from the living, namely, relative permanence of shape and structure, that makes the artificial so effectual a bond between evanescent life forms, and links successive phases of a group into an enduring and progressive community.

In the sphere of technics, once an invention has been made, that task, with rare exceptions, has been done for ever. Thenceforward men may improve upon the work—they have no need to do it afresh. Lesser men may afterwards make and use far superior tools, but only because the product of the inventor's experience has become theirs. Given the fact of society and artificial works, small wonder that material progress occurs so often; what is more remarkable is that such progress is sometimes imperceptible or even absent. Similarly in the field of pure science, our knowledge of the world has reached its imposing proportions, not because our scientists are more able than Ptolemy and Archimedes, but because such men as these were able to give the results of their labours an indestructible form. Nowadays we are better informed than the greatest of the ancients. We are nearer to Life's secrets than Aristotle or Harvey or Buffon. These, and a great host of the known and unknown, have left us a dynamic heritage— the ever growing body of present knowledge and achievement in many fields, and a static heritage—their history, the story of their lives. Our debt to both, and to the artificial which plays so important a part in the transaction, is beyond all reckoning.

CHAPTER VI

The Form of the Instrument

Up to the present we have considered the tool chiefly in relation to its user, to the animal or man or society that employs it. Now let us observe instruments apart from these special relations; let us consider them as material objects that have attributes inseparable from their essence and individuality, and especially characteristic forms. In the history of philosophy the term *form* has come to include many different notions, only one of which need concern us here. According to Aristotle, two intrinsic properties belong to all concrete things—matter and form. That out of which an object is made is its matter; its form is the determining principle which actuates matter and constitutes it a definite kind of being. Without form nothing can exist or be known; it is by their forms that we are aware of things. So the unhewn marble is the matter, and the statue is the form into which that matter is made. Forms make the material of the world into individual things, into appearances which are distinguishable from one another.

Without involving ourselves in the deeper metaphysical problems which surround the concept of form, let us try to throw a little light upon the forms of things artificial, upon the arrangement of their matter, by an empirical method of examination. Before coming to consider the forms of tools it will be helpful to examine the forms of some objects that are not artificial, and in particular the forms of living creatures.

Our first example is an ideal form such as is never found in nature. Consider any parallelopiped of homogeneous material—an ordinary squared log of wood approximates to this condition. If it is supported at both ends it becomes a beam. Its own weight will cause it to assume a more or less curved form, and this distortion is increased by loading the beam in the centre. Here we have, then, a change of form due in the first place to the force of gravity acting downwards and the reactions at the supports, due, in short, to the particular environment of the beam. But external forces are not the sole determinants of the form which the beam has now assumed. There are also the internal forces of resistance set up inside the beam, such as the tensile stresses in the lower part and the compressive stresses in the upper part of the beam's material. The curved form is due to two sets of factors—the external and the internal, to the incidence of outside forces and to the stress and strain within the material itself. In this case, therefore, the new form of the object is determined by the interaction of exterior and interior influences, or, put in another way, it depends upon the nature of the object and the nature of the circumstances in which the object is found.

It is evident that, if we had chosen a beam made of less resistant stuff, its deflection would have been greater, or the beam might possibly have failed under the strain. On the other hand, a stronger material would have deflected less. In these differences of behaviour we see, as it were, the individuality of the material asserting itself within its restricted limits. Supposing that, instead of taking a beam of homogeneous material, we had loaded one made in part of a weaker kind of stuff, one that contained a flaw, this defect would have been made evident under the strain of the load. The symmetry of the beam's curve would have been upset. Similarly, if the beam, though of homogeneous material, had been of irregular shape, the effect of this irregularity would have been seen in the curve under the load.

The object which we have taken as an example is certainly at the mercy of circumstance; it is dominated by its environment; but *exactly* how it will behave under the given conditions will be decided by its inherent qualities no less than by external events. Whether the beam bends little or much, whether it bends symmetrically or asymmetrically, whether it breaks or remains intact—these matters are determined not by external conditions alone, but by a resolution of both, by the interaction of the beam with its world. And since no material object can be exactly the same as any other, and no set of circumstances can ever be entirely repeated, we can never tell with complete precision just how anything—not even an inanimate object—is going to behave. We are able of course, when designing a girder, to assume that materials are perfectly homogeneous, shapes perfectly regular, loads exactly applied, and so forth, and thus to arrive at conclusions which are probably not far from correct. The fact remains, however, that the reaction of a material object to an outward influence is unpredictable since no human mind can ever grasp the entire concrete situation.

Here is adaptation to environment—understood in a certain sense, a fitting in, a response of subject to object, not a purposive adaptation to foreseen circumstances, but a direct consequence of the impact of those circumstances, a direct resolution of internal and external influences. (Lest there should arise any confusion between this kind of adaptation and that kind which organisms show, it will be best to call the former *modification*.) Sometimes the external factor, sometimes the internal, will appear as dominant; but in every case and at every moment each is active, each is a determinant in the history of the object in question, and together they find expression in its form. Let us take an example where the character of the object appears uppermost in the determination of its form. A crystal growing gradually in an evaporating solution will follow more or less the form characteristic of its material. The crystals, however, will not be free from irregularities imposed from outside, such as those which are consequent upon the accidental configuration of the surface upon which crystallization takes place. And external conditions must be ripe for the formation of crystals—in particular, the solution must be saturated. Here environment plays an important part, but the form of the crystal proceeds more especially from the nature of the substance held in solution. As an example of the opposite kind, where external circumstances appear as dominant, consider a volume of water poured into a vessel of some definite shape; the configuration of the liquid now conforms perfectly to the shape of the vessel. It is moulded by outside circumstance. But even here the peculiar character of our material shows itself unmistakeably. Only its fluidity makes possible its new form. And its wetness, or surface-tension, gives rise to the upward curve about the edges of its surface. Had our liquid been mercury, the curve would have been reversed, and a solid, of course, would have remained apparently unaffected.

All things are to some extent plastic; without plasticity they cannot have existence. Again, all things are to some extent self-determinative, having existence from themselves. This is an inescapable duality, of the very essence of being. An object reflects the world, more especially what we may loosely term its world, and reflects this world in its own way. A bending beam pictures for us vividly the forces that deflect it. Invisible forces find visible expression, but the evidence or expression, in this case the form of the beam, is in part the product of the medium which, even in its passivity, contributes something of its own quality. A less resistant material would have been broken, a more resistant would have revealed scarcely a sign of its environment.

Living things are not absolved from this law of direct modification. They also suffer physical change dictated by the immediate circumstance, and suffer it each in his own way. But a further and different principle of adaptation is seen when we come to consider animate forms—a pre-adaptation, a fitting beforehand of the individual for circumstances which he is likely to encounter, in a way that is quite unknown in the inanimate world. This latter kind of adaptation, which has the appearance of being purposive, is of an entirely different order, immeasurably more complex in its manifestations. But both kinds have certain characters in common. The slowly changing form of a genealogical series of living creatures cannot be interpreted as wholly determined by environment, nor as wholly proceeding from the creature, from some internal formative principle. It proceeds, like the form of the inanimate object, from the constant interaction between internal and external influences. If we accept the theory of Natural Selection, then it is clear that a series of organisms has produced its own variations and mutations—these proceed from itself, but environment selects those modified types which alone shall survive and transmit their forms to succeeding generations. Thus the form of a member of any species is the product of the age long interaction between its ancestors and their environments. In the determination of its form the conserved past of its ancestors is operative. And this is where vital adaptation differs from immediate modification—the former is the work of a long past, an undissipated, conserved and organized past; the latter is the product of forces that are unorganized in respect of the thing modified. The changing environment of ages and the organisms' responses of ages—these two, compounded into an indivisible unity, inform the growing foetus. The result, though both the creature and its parent are quite innocent of foresight or any deliberate provision for the future, is that the developing organism is adapted to its probably future environment. Long before it can have any use for them, it grows the organs of sense and the locomotory apparatus of which it is destined, if it survives, to make use of in the outside world. It is adapted in advance to innumerable contingencies, by virtue of the use it makes, all unconsciously, of the experience of its progenitors.

The relations of the organism to its environment are manifold, and it has specialized organs for dealing with special aspects of its world, as the eye for registering the forms that lie within its field, the ear for detecting sounds, the legs for travelling the earth, the hand for grasping the things that the eye has seen. Each of these organs is fitted to that part of the world with which it has to do. The eye is fitted for the reception of light waves, the ear for detecting sound waves, the feet for treading the earth, the hand for holding. To its own special set of circumstances the organ is adapted; it is moulded by them and reflects their character. But this subservience to nature is but half the story. Life fits its organs to their circumstances in its own way, a way that cannot be predicted from any prior examination of the circumstances in question. Life has created its own forms, while in so doing it has of necessity played according to the strict rules of the game, and adapted every organ to its world.

Now one of the most noticeable peculiarities of living things is their symmetry. [1] Not all animals, and certainly not all plants, have forms that are roughly balanced about some axis, but there is a marked tendency towards symmetrical form among Life's arrangements of her material. So universal are these arrangements, that, if we are told of some animal that has the power of active progression, then, without any further information, we may hazard several statements about the form of this creature, and these statements are unlikely to prove far from correct. Assume first that the animal is approaching

---

1   The symmetry of which we speak is of course not an ideal or mathematical symmetry, but only an imperfect approximation to the ideal. In vegetative forms especially is this so.

the point where we are standing. We shall see a figure that is symmetrical about a vertical plane; on one side of a plane passing through the centre of gravity of the figure, lies a shape that is the reverse (or mirror-image) of the shape on the other side. But the shape of the animal is balanced about no horizontal plane; the upper part of the animal is quite different from the lower. Now supposing that we shift our position and view the animal from the side. Here we can trace no symmetry at all. But the back view has, like the front, a symmetry about a vertical plane; the view from above looking downwards reveals a balance about a vertical plane, and the view from beneath has a similar balance. Of the vast majority of animals these observations are true—a fact which may be tested by taking a number of examples.

How is it that most active organisms conform to these rules of symmetry and asymmetry? The answer is simply that they are adapted to their environments. An environment that is, for the organism, balanced, is accompanied by a balanced organization; one that is asymmetrical accompanies an asymmetrical organization. Examine, for example, the human form. As before, we find:-

1. Front view—Symmetry about a vertical plane only.

2. Side view—No symmetry.

3. Rear view—Symmetry about a vertical plane only.

4. View from above—Symmetry about a vertical plane only

5. View from below—Symmetry about a vertical plane only

So much for the form of the man. Now consider his environment, *as it exists* for him. When a man moves through the world, or, what is practically the same thing, as the world flows past him, it does not approach from one side rather than from the other. His relations to things on one hand are not in important respects, nor in the long run, very different from his relations to the things that lie on the other hand. Environment on the left approximates to environment on the right. And the man is organized accordingly. His body is symmetrical about the same plane as his environment. It would be mistaken, of course, to say that the symmetry of the body is entirely *due* to the symmetry of its environment, for the organism, in its movements, is constantly changing one set of circumstances for another, so rendering the entire result symmetrical in the long run. The man does something to maintain this balance by his own mobility and by his own balance of form. If he were to present an asymmetrical front to life, then his environment would be for him one sided, unbalanced. Thus the organism and its environment, in a sense, make one another. Similarly, when we consider the human form in side view, there is no difference, in actual fact, between the world that a man faces, and the world that he leaves behind him; the difference, *for him,* lies in his different relations to these two worlds. The one he is organized to confront, to see, to manipulate; the other he is organized to ignore. Here the organism creates for itself the asymmetry of its environment, just as, from the other viewpoint, it created the symmetry of its environment.

The symmetry of natural forms, wherever it is found, is with few exceptions about a vertical plane. Only occasionally do we find a balance about a horizontal axis. And the reason is not far to seek.

Imagine a plane drawn through the centre of the earth—it will bisect the earth and the atmosphere into approximately equal parts. But another plane at right angles to this vertical plane, and passing near to the surface of the earth, will have to one side of it the earth, to the other, the earth's atmosphere—it will divide its surroundings into two unequal portions. By no scheming can the organism contrive to render this inequality void, save by assuming a spherical form and rolling along. If it remains erect, holding one portion of its body always above the rest, then its environment above is always different from its environment below, and the creature is adapted accordingly. It is asymmetrical; it has accepted one of the data of nature and conformed to it.

If, then, we were to know the nature of any given conditions in detail, that knowledge alone would not enable us to make any predictions concerning the symmetry or asymmetry of any creature living within those conditions. It would be necessary also to know how the creature shifts in this world, whether it moves always with one front presented to the world, whether it travels in one direction relative to its body or in several directions. We must know, in short, something of its relations to its world. But when we have this information, then it is possible to predict with some degree of certitude, not the actual form of the body, but its axes of symmetry. This we may do by applying the following rules:-

1. When the relations between an organism, and its environment lying to one side of a plane passing through the creature's body, are on the average equal to the relations between the organism and the

environment lying to the other side of this plane, then the organism's body tends to be symmetrical about that plane.

2. When these relations are unequal, then the organism tends to be asymmetrical about that plane.

It need hardly be pointed out that we have, in these rules, no key to the actual details of the form which a race of creatures has adopted in a given environment. Bergson has said, 'The circumstances are not a mould into which life is inserted and whose form life adopts: this is indeed to be fooled by a metaphor. There is no form yet, and life must create a form for itself, suited to the circumstances which are made for it. It will have to make the best of these circumstances, neutralize their inconveniences and utilize their advantages—in short, respond to outer actions by building up a machine which has no resemblance to them. Such adapting is not *repeating,* but *replying*—an entirely different thing. If there is still adaptation, it will be in the sense in which one may say of the solution of a problem of geometry, for example, that it is adapted to the conditions. I grant indeed that adaptation so understood explains why different evolutionary processes result in similar forms:- the same problem, of course, calls for the same solution.' [2] In our case, the problem is the symmetry of environments about vertical planes and their lack of symmetry about horizontal ones. And this problem has called for the same solution among the majority of mobile animals.

As the human body is adapted to its environment, so also are its organs adapted to their own environments. The arm has for

---

2   *Creative Evolution,* Eng. Trans., p. 61

environment at one extremity the shoulder, at the other the changing world. This difference is reflected in its lack of symmetry; it is *inflected*. Likewise the head and legs are inflected towards the trunk to which they are joined. The fingers are rounded at one extremity and furnished with nails, which are adaptations to an environment totally different from that which lies at the other extremity—they are inflected towards the hand. Again, the hand as a whole is inflected towards the wrist and laterally towards the body—its dependence upon the trunk is reflected in its form. Almost every part of the body will be found to indicate by its shape the nature of its environment.

Living forms that are endowed with no locomotory apparatus of their own remain to be considered. Take, for example, a tree. Supposing there is no prevailing wind, that winds blow as often and as hard from one quarter as from another, supposing also that environment is in all other ways equal on all sides of a growing tree, even under such impossible conditions a tree would never be, even to the most casual glance, perfectly symmetrical about a vertical axis; nevertheless it would approximate to this condition. But about a horizontal axis there will be no tendency towards symmetry, for the same reason that there is none amongst animals. Each branch is inflected towards the main stem; each leaf is inflected towards its twig; each flower is inflected towards its stem. Every part of the tree, whether great or small, shows in its form its dependence upon the whole. The shape of every organ proclaims that it exists from the whole and for the whole. The function of every organ is to mediate between the world and the organism to which it belongs;

between these two spheres the organ operates, and it is adapted to them respectively. But among plants, as we have already noticed, individuality is often loose, therefore we must not expect a very strict adherence to the rule of inflection. The reader will readily recall a number of exceptions.

Man's artificial works are the links and adaptive devices whereby he fits the world and his body together, the means for maintaining and progressively changing his biological relations to this world. The artificial organ, like the natural one, is a mediator between man and circumstance. We may expect to find, therefore, that the forms of instruments show adaptation to the exterior world on the one hand, and to the human user on the other, while they are governed also by internal necessities of their constitutions.

Let us take a few simple examples, and, to begin with, an ordinary claw-hammer. This is a kind of three-way tool. It is specially adapted to three unlike portions of its normal field—the shaft to the human hand, the head to the nail that has to be driven, and the claw to the nail that has to be extracted. The weight, the shape and the material of the head, and the length and diameter of the handle, all follow from this threefold environment. But the form of the joint between these two parts must be traced to the nature of the materials of the tool and to the forces acting with it, rather than to the nature of the nails that are hit and drawn, or to the hand that wields, and the design of every part is governed to some degree by the materials of which it is made. Outside conditions, however, dominate the pattern of the tool. The hammer, like the arm it extends, is inflected towards the organism that uses it—the asymmetry of its environment is reflected in the asymmetry of its form. But in end view the hammer is symmetrical just as, from this aspect, its environment is in the long run asymmetrical. All the organs of man, whether artificial or natural, follow the same laws of symmetry and inflection.

For our next example we will take a more complex tool, such as a railway locomotive and train. The world flows past the train in one direction only; environment before is not for the moving train the same as environment behind. Accordingly, the fore part of the locomotive that fronts the onrushing world, and the guard's van that brings up the rear, are differentiated. The train is inflected along the line of its motion; it has direction of form, like the self propelling animal. And the front and rear views of the train are, of course, symmetrical—here environment is balanced. Turning now to the parts of the train, we may notice that the lower extremity is adapted to its own environment, namely, the rails, and is furnished with wheels. The uppermost part has to deal with totally different conditions and needs a curved roof to throw off the rain. Each part of the train, down to the last belt, observes the laws of inflection and symmetry, with certain partial exceptions. As an example of imperfect adaptation the funnel will serve; it if were strictly adapted it would be stream-lined, inflected in the direction of its motion, but it remains circular. Among artefacts, as among organisms, there is no hard and fast observance of formal rules.

For our third example let us take a somewhat different kind of human work—a building. It will be seen that buildings present a problem somewhat different from that of the simple hand tool, in that they have for us two aspects, an external and an internal. They have enveloped, so to speak, a portion of their environments, and are adapted internally as well as externally to human requirements. If an architect is commissioned to design a theatre, he has to envisage the human action which will take place inside it. Whatever plan is adopted, the stage properties, the actors, the orchestra and the audience, must be ranged in sequence. The principal action within the building operates in this direction—from proscenium to auditorium, and determines the main axis of the theatre. About this axis the structure will be roughly symmetrical; along this axis the structure will have 'direction'. But about another axis normal to the last, there can be no symmetry. On one side the actors must be accommodated, for them the dressing rooms, the green room and the stage must be provided; on the other side are the pit, the gallery and the boxes, the staircases and the foyer. There can be no attempt to balance such different requirements. And so the typical theatre has axes of symmetry which correspond with those of the mobile animal. It has 'direction'; it is deliberately inflected, not in respect of its own motion—for it has none, but in respect of the direction of the motion within.

This fact of purpose, of deliberate design, makes the adaptation of the artificial of an entirely different order from the adaptation of the organism, and from the direct modification of bodies by environment. Only of the works of a reasonable being can we safely say that they are devised with a foreknowledge of the circumstances likely to be brought to bear upon them. Certainly the organism does not by taking thought plan its own structure, and the ancient belief that creatures have been adapted by intelligent but miraculous agencies is clearly founded upon an anthropomorphic argument. Man is the only intelligent adaptor of which we have conclusive evidence. He alone is able to hold in mind the given circumstances, then to devise an object adapted to those circumstances, and finally to give shape to the adapted article. In his mind the outward conditions and response play upon each other till a clear idea of the eventual form is achieved. But however different the artificial method of adaptation is from the natural, the results of each have much in common. The form of the artificial organ, because it is fitted to the same order of conditions as the natural organ, and exists for the same purpose, has the same general characters as the form of living structures. The technician unwittingly observes the same rules of form as Life. His utilitarian works have a formal configuration that is reminiscent of Nature's.

Mr. Trystan Edwards has produced two books [3] dealing with what he calls a Grammar of Design, and this Grammar consists of three formal canons called respectively, Number, Punctuation and Inflection. To these canons, says Mr. Trystan Edwards, all organisms conform, and he would have designers, and architects in particular, pay attention to these principles of good composition. If they do so we are assured that buildings, and indeed all works composed in accordance with his recommendations, will have 'life', though never so much vitality, he is careful to add, as even the most primitive organisms.

---

3   *The Things which are Seen* & *Architectural Style.*

We will briefly review Mr. Trystan Edwards' cannons. The first is Number. Nature abhors a duality, contrives always that two nearly similar parts of an organism shall be resolved into an inclusive unity. Living things have many organs that are arranged in pairs, as eyes, legs, wings and horns, but such organs are shaped so that each is plainly part of a whole. The human hand and foot, for example, draw attention by their lack of symmetry to the hand and foot on the other side of the body, and do not constitute centres of interest in themselves. They are dominated by the pattern of the whole. Among all natural forms which are nearly symmetrical, their symmetry is not that of two competing units but of two parts, either of which by its own lack of balance suggests the other.

Mr. Trystan Edwards' second canon is that of Punctuation. He finds that the boundaries of organisms have a 'formal emphasis', some mark that here, at the extremity of the form, we have done with it. And he ventures the statement that 'it will be found that punctuation is a mark of beauty and that the higher an organism may be in the scale of life, the more subtly are its parts punctuated.' The leg of a horse is punctuated by the hoof; a lion's tail is punctuated by the tuft of hair at the end of it, and so on throughout nature.

The final canon is Inflection, with which we have already made some acquaintance. A part of an organism shows sensitiveness to its surroundings; by its shape it refers one to the whole, it makes a formal recognition of the rest of the body. And, similarly, the shape of the body as a whole makes a formal recognition of its environment.

With most of this we heartily agree. The three canons of design are nothing but a restatement of the facts of adaptation. Mr. Trystan Edwards has noticed the formal results of the interaction of environment and organism, and has elaborated his discoveries into three rules—somewhat arbitrarily into three, for they are but parts of one grand principle. But precisely because he has failed thoroughly to appreciate this underlying law—that the forms of living things are merely the outward evidence of their adjustment to conditions, he has contrived to put his admirable canons to illegitimate uses. He has set them up as rules of good taste to which those who design utilitarian structures should pay respect, even when these rules appear to be at variance, in some measure, with functional requirements. Mr. Edwards has taken the letter of the law and ignored its spirit. Having observed the results of strict adaptation in nature, he would use his interpretation of those results to obstruct strict utilitarian adaptation in artifice. One quotation will make this clear. 'The chapters on the Grammar of Design', says Mr. Edwards, referring to the earlier part of his book, 'show clearly how even in objects usually manufactured by the engineer the canons of composition can be observed, and these agreeable excellences of form would not be arrived at by an observance of constructional needs alone. Of course it is true that in certain instances, notably in those appertaining to the canon of punctuation, the rounding off happens to coincide with structural convenience, *but this is merely an accident...* A stone column generally has a capital of some sort in order to spread the pressure, but in concrete piers the capital is often omitted because not constructionally necessary. But how crude and unsatisfactory a support becomes if it has neither base nor capital! It is found, then, that sometimes, by accident, the engineer may give effect to the canon of punctuation. Of the other canons—of number and inflection—he takes no cognizance whatever.' [4]

Now a man who designs intricate machines, if he is worthy of the task, designs scientifically. He puts no frills upon his work. He is content to produce a structure that is, as far as possible, adapted to its environment. Every part of the thing he builds is of necessity made of this shape, of that material; there is practically no latitude of design; all is governed by the strict necessities of the case. His business is to design, as we say, functionally. If he oversteps the bounds of his province, as he sometimes does, then he is acting no longer in the capacity of engineer and has turned 'artist'. As engineer, however, he has no business with canons of good taste, no rules of design for agreeable effects, no ideal proportions at which to aim. Active aestheticism can only be for him an impediment to his proper activity. But by rigid adherence to utility does the engineer often flagrantly disobey the canons of design that we find exemplified in nature? By strictly adapting every part does the technician outrage the dictates of good taste, or stumble perhaps by merest accident upon a felicitous arrangement? So, it appears, Mr. Trystan Edwards would have us believe. Such a conclusion could not be further from the truth. It is rather the artist, or the engineer turned artist, who is liable by his modifications of the utilitarian structure to blunt its adaptive

---

4   *The Things which are Seen*, p. 245. (Italics mine.)

subtleties, impair its usefulness, and add unmeaning embellishments to what has already the organic 'rightness' of a carefully adapted mechanism. The work that is at every point determined by practical conditions observes, *ipso facto,* the same formal rules as the organism that is similarly adapted, though not necessarily to Mr. Trystan Edwards' liking.

But, in actual fact, not all of the structures which the engineer designs are so completely adapted. A great part of his work proceeds by methods that are as yet unscientific, by rule of thumb and empirical formulae. In addition, it often happens that there are several equally efficient solutions of one problem. In short, the engineer has some latitude of operation. At this point—where there are alternative solutions—the engineer is liable to construct forms that are unpleasing, that contravene our canons. And here it is that the artist may render valuable service, not indeed by interfering with the strictly determined forms of the engineer, but by choosing where opportunity for choice exists, by preventing the addition of unsuitable ornament, and sometimes by 'humanizing' the correct but bleak utilitarian work. The artist may think fit to modify or to add ornament to the bare useful object. Such deviations from the engineer's standards may often be practised with advantage in order to emphasize subtleties of form and to give an added human interest to the work. But—and this is the important thing to notice—if it is indeed a work conceived and executed by the scientific type of mind, moulded in every part by inescapable circumstances, then no addition of ornament, no concealment of structure, no modification of form demanded by the artist, will improve upon the formal correctness which follows from thorough adaptation. If an engineering work is incorrectly inflected, it is so because the designer has fallen short of his own standards, not those of the artist.

The truth of these statements may be confirmed by taking a few examples from those works of the engineer with which the artist, as such, has had little or nothing to do. The vehicles that are built especially for racing—aeroplanes, cars, speed-boats; and all the lamentably efficient engines of destruction—warships, bombing planes, submarines, guns, rifles; as well as countless instruments employed by scientists and technicians: in all such forms there may be traced a beauty that is not the beauty of the work of art, but of the same order as the beauty of organisms. It is the beauty—I would prefer the term *rightness* or satisfactoriness of form—which attends the organization of parts into wholes that work. It is the orderliness which is found wherever organs function economically. To study these quasi-natural forms, to derive inspiration from them as he does from nature, is the prerogative of the artist. For him to play a part in their making would be to rob them of those very qualities which he finds so stimulating.

Examine carefully the general shape of an aeroplane, note the articulation of its members, the dominance of the whole over every part, the nice inflection of the wings and tail, the formal direction of the machine along its line of flight and the symmetry of its plan. Turn to the smaller parts, examine in order every lever, every pipe, every strut and tie, and you will find that everywhere there is a subtle harmony of forms. If we were to probe into the interior parts of the engine, still we should find it. Here are formal graces that the artist may well admire. The warship too, unlovely though its purpose is, displays the same formal rectitude. Everything down to the colour of its paint is determined, not by good taste, but by necessity, with the result that the most fastidious taste is satisfied. But to labour the point further is unnecessary. The reader may discover countless examples for himself.

The machine, then, is not a work of art, for the obvious reason that the free imagination plays no part in its design. Nor is it necessarily beautiful. Just as some organisms are thought ugly, so some machines, formally correct though they be, are generally thought to be of unpleasant shape. For beauty can never be achieved by the observance of rules. The artist adopts certain limitations, but you cannot measure the value of his work by the mould into which it is fitted. If art could be reduced to rules, then mere application of formulae would serve to render a man an artist, and art would become a mere technique.

CHAPTER VII

Nature and the Artificial in Art

'Only when he plays is a man really and truly a man', says Schiller, with some exaggeration. But certainly any account of the works of man which omitted to mention the vast field of artifice which is, biologically speaking, quite useless to him, would be misleading indeed. Man's superior intelligence, his habit of conceptual thought and reason, his moral sense, and, above all, his appreciation of beauty, lift him right out of the sphere of the biologist. He appears as a soul, and as such he has needs, even material needs, which cannot be explained without reference to his higher activities. He remains still a body, and so must have his complement of utilitarian instruments, living and dead. The mind also is in part a 'biologically' useful tool whereby these instruments may be devised, maintained and improved. But it is more. There is nothing known which man cannot contemplate for its own sake, utterly without regard to its use for him. There are many things in the world that he alters just because it pleases him to do so, though his bodily life is in no way made more comfortable by the alteration. The earth is full of things which he has made, simply because they appear admirable to him or pleasant to make, to hear or to look upon. Even the most utilitarian action may be performed, in part or entirely, for the sake of the performance. The deed is delightful quite apart from the thing done. The astronomer who devotes his life to the study of the remotest star clusters, the theologian who attempts to discover the nature of God, the painter and the musician striving to express what is dimly imagined but strongly felt, the amateur footballer and the child at play, are all engaged in pursuits which are of no material benefit to the community, though they are often of material benefit to the individuals concerned. It is the completeness with which man gives himself up to these things that differentiates him, more than anything else, from the rest of animals.

An important principle must now be observed. In our hierarchy of 'organisms', the 'useful' activity of a subordinate individual often appears of indifferent value or even detrimental to the individual at a higher level. For example, the immediate welfare of any part of the bodily tissue, if we may so term its growth, is not necessarily the welfare of the organism as a whole. Again, writing poems is occasionally profitable to poets, but it is not so to society. The destruction or injury of an organ occasionally benefits the organism, and similarly, to despoil an individual of his extensions, even to remove him altogether, is in certain cases to the community's advantage. When, therefore, we speak of some science and all art, religion and play as useless activities, and of works of art and the instruments of religion and play as useless objects, it is understood that we are regarding these from a social and not from an individual standpoint. A work of art made for gain, a church built for profit and designed for fees, a game played by professionals, are biologically useless performances to all except those who earn money by them. Put in general terms, the 'utility' of behaviour and structure is relative to the level from which these are viewed.

It has often been maintained that what we call very primitive art was pursued for didactic and magical ends; its real or supposed purpose was biological utility of some kind. But there seems little reason to doubt that the work gave pleasure in the making, and it is certain that a great many primitive *objets d'art* have been most imaginatively conceived. Whatever the solution to these problems, from remote times till now all forms of art activity have scarcely ever been free from practical motives of one kind or another. Thus, art objects are bought and sold, the talent that makes them is for sale in the market-place, the wealthy surround themselves with valuable and beautiful works largely on account of the prestige they bring, commerce presses the artist into its service to help sell its commodities, and even the most scrupulous of artists tries to make a living. In addition, vast numbers of true works of art contain propaganda, point morals, give information, and make wise or unwise observations of every sort.

Religion, that other great 'useless' activity, is mixed in much the same way with useful or ostensibly useful intentions and results. It is nearly always a means of livelihood for its ministers; it may sometimes be the bulwark of a dominant class against oppressed and superstitious masses, as Marx believed. And its effects upon conduct, whether for good or ill, are of course more or less proportional to the intensity of faith that it inspires. Games and play of all kinds, too, have their obvious biological effects. In fact, it would not be an exaggeration to say of all human activities which are of no direct use to the community as a whole, that they are materially profitable to some section of it, that many such activities are indirectly beneficial to the community at large, and that each of them affects profoundly every other activity in society. In spite of such complications, however, the essential quality of art, pure science, religion and play, is that these activities are performed for their own sakes, or rather on account of the mental satisfaction they yield. Whatever biological uses these have, their utility is secondary and contingent only. The prominent feature of these occupations is that they are *free,* dominated by no practical necessity. Their works, if they are tools at all, are mental ones, and not instruments of the body.

We find, then, that a great deal of human behaviour is, from the biologist's viewpoint, quite superfluous, that many of the artificial organs of humanity have embellishments that do not make them more efficient, and that besides these partly useful organs are material human works that are entirely valueless in the struggle for life. Does this state of affairs find no reflection elsewhere in the stream of life? Is this exuberance a sudden affair which appears only with man, his own invention and prerogative? Or is it the outcropping of a tendency that has been present, though in a latent form, from the beginnings of life? Can this apparent unconcern with the hard struggle for existence, this partial freedom both in behaviour and organization from necessity, this temporary relief from the urgencies of hunger and love, be traced here and there under different guises in the lives of other creatures?

I think it can; but it does not appear, of course, as art in the accepted sense of the term. But play is certainly to be found. Spencer regarded play as a spontaneous discharge of excessive energy that, having no serious work in hand, is released in simulated instead of real actions. [1] The play of young animals is also in part a preparation for adult life; nevertheless it is an activity free from immediate practical issues. The elaborate courtships of birds, though it has for end the most practical of all functions, is a long way round to that conclusion. But what shall we say of the play of adult birds, of their throw-and-catch games [2], of their curious flights which seem to have some of the thrill of circus aerobatics about them, and of their communal drill and dances? To all appearances these things are done out of sheer exhilaration, as pure play with no other end in view save the enjoyment of the game itself.

But just as much animal behaviour has no direct utility, so there are in nature many organs which have, as far as it is possible to say, no practical value for their owners. Life is a matter of instruments, the means whereby death is avoided, but not all of the structures which Life produces are adapted towards such utilitarian ends. Some have a usefulness that is indirect only; some have lost their once useful functions and yet remain as worthless or definitely harmful luggage to be borne by the organism; some, once useful, have continued to flourish beyond the bounds of the strict requirements of their

1   *Principles of Psychology,* Part IX, Chap.IX.
2   See Julian Huxley, *Essays of a Biologist.*

possessors and have become a menace; some appear never to have had any biological use whatever. Let us glance for a moment at some of these extravagances in Nature's economy.

We have noticed in a previous chapter the persistence of vestigial organs, how, for instance, a flightless bird may still retain vestiges of its once adequate wings, how the whale still has, in a very reduced form, the hind limbs which it formerly used for locomotion. There is no great difficulty in accounting for these degenerate organs, but another kind of structure which is quite as useless as these, presents a more serious problem to the biologist. The skeletons of many species of Radiolaria and Foraminifera consist of intricate symmetrical patterns that are often remarkably beautiful, but though a framework of some kind is no doubt necessary, it seems highly improbable that detail of one type can be more efficacious than another in the struggle for life. And throughout nature there are innumerable devices that seem to indicate an inventiveness, pursued as though its creations were valuable in themselves, an offshoot from the purely practical. No doubt many of the factors leading up to these phenomena will yield somewhat to research, and adaptive characters will be discovered where now we see what appears to be mere ornament, but there is likely to remain a great body of facts which cannot be so interpreted.

Among higher organisms we find such curious organs as the helmet of the hornbill and the huge bony plates along the back of the extinct reptile Stegosaurus. To account for these, it has been suggested that natural selection may at first have favoured those members of a species that were deficient in the hormones which regulated the growth of the organs in question, and that, after a long period of selection, the glands which secreted these hormones ceased to do so. There then remained no check to the growth of such organs beyond the limits of utility. [3] Perhaps preferential mating may have had something to do with these grotesque characters— it has certainly been responsible for a great deal of the 'ornament' that is to be found in nature. Hen birds of many species have, in the course of countless generations, actually 'designed' their males. By the simple process of choosing the more attractive for mates they have collectively demonstrated their preferences in form and colour. And the interesting thing about their choice is that it seems to be in accord with our own. Darwin writes: 'I willingly admit that a great number of male animals, as all our most gorgeous birds, some fishes, reptiles, and mammals, and a host of magnificently coloured butterflies, have been rendered beautiful for beauty's sake; but this has been effected through sexual selection, that is, by the more beautiful males having been continually preferred by the females, and not for the delight of man. So it is with the music of birds. We may infer from all this that a nearly similar taste for beautiful colours and for musical sounds runs through a large part of the animal kingdom.' [4] The mere passive choice of a few alternatives, and that so mixed with biological motives, is, however, a long way from art as we understand it.

There are a few curious instances of what appears to be deliberate ornamentation in nature. A well known case is that of the bower-bird which decorates its run with gay feathers, rags, bones, shells, and

3   Sir Arthur Dendy, *Evolutionary Biology,* p. 425
4   *Origin of Species,* Chap.VI

other white or brilliant objects. This certainly suggests the rudiments of art, but it may well be that this instinct once had its practical use and that it has undergone some modification that has rendered it valueless. If this should be so, then the instinct persists in much the same way as the vestigial organ. The decorated run, in fact, would be a vestigial organ of the bird's extended body, much as skeuomorphic decoration is of man's.

We have taken enough evidence to show that the behaviour and structure of every organism is not in every way strictly utilitarian. The action and reaction of environment and organism have provoked, as it were, by-products in life's industry. The distinctions between these by-products in our own life and in the life of other animals are as great as the distinctions between our own minds and theirs, and consist of differences both in kind and degree. Nevertheless the bodily organization of man, his artificial additions to this, his behaviour and his works of art, all belong to the great structure of life. They are not detached from it, but spring, like the turrets of a great building, from the foundations in which the form of the superstructure may be traced in outline, though never in detail. Man, as we have observed before, is evolution's heir. He is taking over more and more the control of his own destiny and with it the destiny of other creatures. In previous chapters we have watched the rapid evolution of his artificial organization and observed the part that artificial organs play in the integration of society. By artifice man has grown outwards and society around him has grown more complex. If for a moment we take an external view of these developments, we find that from the core outwards every layer of his greater body is in part utilitarian and in part 'free'. Man's body, its artificial extensions, the organs of society, and lastly the untouched environment, all display this overplus as far as he is concerned, this partial freedom from organic necessity that we have noticed in the organization of some of the lower organisms. Man, regarded organically, merges by easy stages with the world, and at every stage, along with the organs of necessity, there are the non-adaptive characters, the free creations of life.

Let us rapidly examine his organic constitution with an eye for useless parts. The human body, as everyone knows, has a number of vestigial organs and several parts—the appendix, for instance—to which the physiologist can attribute no useful function. To these non-adaptive characters man himself has added a very different kind. Europeans shave, trim the hair, and distort the body in many ways, but some primitive peoples have taken the art of body-design much further, going to great lengths to improve, as it is thought, upon nature. Nowhere is man quite content with the body he inherits but in some way or other he refashions it to his taste. Then there are the exterior fashions. The successful warrior supplies himself with badges of skill; teeth and bones are worn as symbols of the slain and of the conqueror's prowess, more than on account of any decorative value these may have. But almost from the first, the arrangement of trophies presented some problems of taste, and here we may detect one of the beginnings of art. Another primitive practice which, though utilitarian, gave great scope for imaginative powers, is that of attempting to terrorize the enemy by painting the features and decking the body with many strange devices. Clothes must be adapted to weather and wearer, but when all such conditions are satisfied, the latitude left for free design is well nigh boundless. Useful tools and weapons have from a very early date been embellished with varying richness. Household furniture, buildings, and the innumerable articles of everyday use about us, nearly all have a touch of free fancy about them—if not ornament, then some modification of form which has not been demanded by practical considerations. Books, too, that are intended for information only and are without literary pretensions, are rarely devoid of some attempt to present edifying material in an appetizing form, just as food is served to appeal to one sense by first ministering to another.

There is no hard and fast line of demarcation between the thing of use to which there has been a conscious attempt to give beauty, and a work performed, as we say, for art's sake. Glass and china and silver find their way from the pantry to the show-case. Building passes over into architecture and architecture into monument-making. Embellishment of the useful, pushed far enough, becomes free creation of the useless. In many unadorned instruments men find aesthetic delight, though such has not been the primary intention of the makers; other objects are deliberately designed to please the eye, though without sacrifice of utility; finally there are the pure works of art, things of no use to the body, that minister only to spiritual needs. Society, reflecting these necessities of the spirit, is organized accordingly. Institutions and groups of men, of which the sole *raison d'être* is the pursuit of art or of some other non-utilitarian practice, are very numerous in any civilized community. And beyond lies the world of nature. In this world man is interested for practical reasons, but not for them alone. He finds that in many of her aspects Nature is for him sublime, wonderful, beautiful. The scientist seeks truth in nature, the artist seeks beauty. Nature, just like the artificial object, has her two aspects for man: she appears as a means to his ends, and as an end in herself.

The burning question is, of course, what is the nature of the aesthetic object and of the aesthetic experience? To what extent does the mind contribute to, or help to constitute, the aesthetic object? The answer which a philosopher gives to these questions depends upon his general affiliations, upon whether he inclines towards the neo-realist or the idealist persuasion. Those of the former school tend to make the object of the aesthetic experience independent of the mind; those of the latter say that it is the object *as enjoyed,* as constituted by the mind. The normative discipline of aesthetics is a favourite field of battle between thinkers of many diverse opinions, and no useful purpose could be served here by attempting to judge between them. It seems as unlikely that agreement will be reached in this department of philosophy as among the underlying doctrines of metaphysics and epistemology that colour all the discussions of aestheticians. As to the psychological nature of the aesthetic experience, whether it is the 'repose of a subject in an object', as Miss E. D. Puffer describes it [5], the objectified pleasure of Santayana [6], the projection of our feelings into an object, as the theories of Einfühlung maintain, the primary

5   *The Psychology of Beauty.*
6   *The Sense of Beauty.*

activity of 'expression' of Croce and his disciple Carrit, or simply imagination:—such questions are altogether beyond the scope of this book and irrelevant to our present purpose.

Let us attack the problem of art from another angle, avoiding the deeper dilemmas, by attempting to set the arts in some kind of order and noting particularly their relation to nature.

The first distinction to be made is between the representational arts, and those which do not usually seek to imitate or to derive direct inspiration from nature. Clearly among the former arts are included literature—comprising prose and poetry, most painting, sculpture, the drama, and the recent arts of photography and the cinema. Among the non-representational are music, architecture, and most of the industrial arts and crafts.

Commencing with the representational arts, we shall find it useful to revert to the table in chapter 4, and to the explanatory matter in the accompanying text. The table gives a list of ways by which aspects of an experience may be communicated, ranging between the spoken description and the film. An event which has actually occurred may, by the various methods mentioned, be re-presented to the enquirer, who uses his imagination to fill out what is lacking in the instrument of communication, so that he obtains a more or less vivid mental picture of the event. Now, each of these modes has, or at one time has had, great practical usefulness. By each of them men have learned about the 'real' world of fact, enlarged their experience of nature and of human affairs to an extent otherwise unattainable. But, though the representations so used are artificial, they are not yet art, except in so far as they are endowed by the representer with certain qualities and especially with a kind of imaginativeness. When these modes of representation are used with a view to giving information about the world as it is, fanciful departures from the business in hand are plainly out of place.

As a matter of fact however, and this is more particularly true of the modes towards the beginning of the table, it is impossible for the representer to keep himself entirely out of the picture. His report has inevitably a personal colour. What he thinks important will dominate his narrative at the expense of what he thinks irrelevant or has failed to notice. In his description of any concrete event he cannot help but select those aspects which strike him most forcibly. There are as many possible histories of eras as there are possible historians, and as many possible biographies of an individual as there are possible biographers. Each who witnesses a concrete series of events has a unique personal history which determines what he shall see and what he shall neglect, and determines accordingly the information he imparts. If his aim, however, is objective truth, then the measure of his success is proportional to the measure of his impartiality; the more he is able to check his own prejudices, personal feelings and imaginations, the more useful his documents; the more he refers all to nature, to what is given, the more reliable his picture.

The distinction between this kind of representation and representational art is profound, yet they merge by imperceptible degrees with one another. The artist's aim is in some respects essentially the reverse of his who desires to communicate knowledge of actual occasions. The artist's primary concern is not with the pure objective or extra-human truth, if, indeed, that could be known; he does not try to avoid but to welcome an imaginative treatment of the object. What he adds to the object and what he neglects, his individual impression of it, the feeling with which his experience is tinged, these are essential in the artist's activity. The work of representational art has not lost all traces of the original external stimulus; it still portrays some exterior fact, but not necessarily with any great faithfulness. Since the work of art is the object as the artist apprehends it and feels about it, it may be—it *must* be—distorted or simplified or modified through and through by the creative imagination.

But mere imagination, you will object, is surely not art. Certainly mere dreaming, mere play of fancy is not yet art, though it is the basis of art. The work of art, to realize its end, namely, the achievement of beauty, must be a whole, an organized unity. A collection of imaginative elements, threaded together, will not arrive at beauty until they are fitted into one another, till each part is subordinated to the whole. If there remain over elements which do not pay respect to the dominant idea, there is that lack of harmony which we call ugliness. To be successful a work of art must be self consistent; every detail must be thoroughly worked into the general scheme, and the particular quality that marks the whole must govern the part that each element plays in the structure. Clearly, then, there can be no definite boundary line between the presentations of the idle, uncritical imagination, and the genuinely beautiful work. Between these two are ranged products of the imagination which lack, to a greater or lesser extent, the coherence of the beautiful whole.

Nor is there any distinct division between the representational work that imitates nature as closely as possible and the highly imaginative work of art. They are the poles of artistic activity. The former cannot be utterly devoid of the imaginative qualities which the latter has in full measure. The difference between them, therefore, is one of degree. But there is also a difference in direction and aim. Representational art gravitates between the extremes of naturalism on one side and fantasy on the other, like a slowly swinging pendulum. The history of art is an account of the motion to and fro between these limits. Always there is movement in one of two directions, either from an unrestricted imagination towards a faithful portrayal of nature, or the reverse. Progress in one direction begins to halt as the goal is approached, and attainment sees the beginning of an advance in the opposite direction. In other words, though the end towards which an art is moving at any time is either extreme realism or extreme 'expressionism', as soon as either of those ends is almost achieved the dynamic tradition has arrived at an impasse, it has defeated its own ends, and can only gain impetus as it recedes from the haven that had before appeared so desirable to the artist. In painting, for example, if a 'photographic' likeness could be made, such a likeness would not be a work of art; if all resemblance to the object portrayed were lost, if the representation were quite irrecognizable, again we would not have a work of representational art, though it might be excellent abstract art. At every point between these poles works of art are to be found, and in every instance the work has a direction either towards the goal of verisimilitude or away from it.

In our first chapter we spoke of degrees of artificiality. The artificial we described as that which proceeds from man; the more behaviour and works are conditioned by unrestricted human impulses, the more artificial they are. On the other hand, activities and their products which are regulated more directly by the requirements of environment, are said to be relatively natural. The freer the activity the more artificial its material works. One of the least restricted and most artificial of human activities is art. It has a measure of independence of nature; it is not rigidly determined; the imagination which inspires it is under no obligation to bow to natural laws or to the appearances of nature. Now it is the essence of the craft of representation for useful purposes that it shall, like any other technical pursuit, defer to exterior circumstance; as the machine must be conformed to nature to conquer her, so the useful document must conform to nature to re-present her. This craft, then, is less artificial than the art of representing imaginatively. So we may say that the ceaseless swinging of the pendulum in the history of art is a fluctuation between what is more artificial and what is less so.

Let us now take the principal arts of representation in turn, noting in each this motion, the inevitable systole and diastole of tradition.

The art of literature is of two kinds, applied and pure—applied, when it is used primarily as a means of communicating information; pure, when the way in which information is set forth becomes more important than the bare meaning of the message. [7] Literature as a pure art is indifferent to fact. It may possibly tell us what is true or useful; nevertheless its status does not rest upon these qualities but upon the quality of the expression achieved. A work judged as literary in this sense, must stand upon its own merits without appeal to outside fact. When we read imaginative poetry such as Coleridge's often quoted *Kubla Khan* or the work of Blake, we do not concern ourselves with such questions as: did Kubla in fact build himself a pleasure-dome in Xanadu, or was the historical Christ actually seen to walk upon England's mountains? The truth or the untruth of the poet's statement is immaterial. What is important is that he shall convey the quality of his imaginative experience, that he shall arouse in us also the feeling that inspired him. Whether he tells us the truth or patent falsehoods (if by falsehoods we mean contradictions of everyday facts), whether he tells us a great deal or scarcely anything at all, affects not at all the aesthetic validity of his work. And sometimes it is unnecessary to thoroughly understand what the writer means in order to appreciate his deeper intention; word-music subtly played is an indispensable vehicle of many imaginative moods.

To judge of the merit of the literary work of art, we must refer to the impulse behind it and to the degree of success with which the author has handled his material of communication. By quite different standards must we judge of the composition that professes to inform

---

7   The status of writing as pure literature does not rest wholly upon what may be termed *style*, of course. By 'the way in which information is set forth' I mean to imply not only the 'form' but also certain aspects of the 'content', as for example the subtle manifold verbal associations which play so important a part in literary creation and appreciation.

us of objective truth, or to serve any practical purpose. Such a work must stand or fall by reference to the validity of its information, and the clarity with which the writer has conveyed his message. Of course it is possible to regard applied literature from the aesthetic angle. Thus many didactic writings appear as true works of art when their practical merits are ignored and their other qualities emphasized. The books of a number of the ancient and modern philosophers, for example, may be enjoyed in either way, and while reading them we may constantly shift from one of these viewpoints to the other.

So in literature there is at one extreme more or less pure imagination, subjective 'nonsense' on all practical showing, and at the other hard fact, or propositions concerning the objective world. Between these limits, between the more and the less artificial, the pendulum must swing. Now just as some biologists stress the influence of environment and others the action of the organism, so some critics stress the importance of the subjective, imaginative, aesthetic side of literary composition, while some of the less orthodox concern themselves more especially with what the author has to say about nature, about what exists or should exist in the outside world. And within this latter school of critics may be detected those who look for an accurate picture of things as they are—for realism, and those who look for propaganda—for a picture of the future and for advice as to how such a future may be brought about.

Two very different writers of this last variety are Mr. C. E. M. Joad [8] and Mr. Upton Sinclair. [9] They appear to agree, however, that if all

8   *Unorthodox Dialogues on Art and Education*
9   *Mammonart*

propaganda is scarcely art, at least the best art is nearly all propaganda with a spoonful of artistic jam to make the medicine palatable. For them art is essentially an instrument of the Life Force or of Social Progress, existing for the disruption of the worn-out order and for heralding the new, rather than for the titillation of aesthetes. And both of them are driven by their doctrine (surely against their wills) to rank Shakespeare a second-rate artist. Into such strange positions does their thesis lead them! [10] But a theory which is not completely shattered by such a grotesque application as this, but continues to reappear in some guise or another, cannot be without a vestige of reason. Obviously, some magnificent prose has been written by men enthusiastic for a cause or an idea, who took, so far as we can see, no conscious thought for literary graces; to say clearly and trenchantly what they must, that was their sole concern. The result may be as truly literary as *Grace Abounding*, or it may be as uninspired as any political or religious pamphlet. The work of men like Shaw and Wells owes, of course, a great deal to their sincerity of purpose. But though unlimited sincerity may move mountains and conquer empires, it cannot write one page of literature unless, as in the works of these famous writers, something more is added. Nor is every brilliant man of letters a prophet or a social reformer. The fact is that both the extreme of realism and the extreme of romanticism are eventually

---

10   The cardinal error of critics of this school seems to be that they regard only the superficial message of the artist, appearing never to realize that the artist, though he may give us no obviously new information, no novel propaganda, no gospel of progress, may yet, though he describes what is already known and obvious, give us unique revelations of the familiar world which subserve profounder purposes than the merely practical and intellectual. The 'Life Force' is surely not concerned solely with progress in the familiar sense, but no less with the expansion of aesthetic sensibilities.

found to be *culs-de-sac*; realism pushed far enough is no longer art; it is devoid of the imaginative qualities which lift literature above scribbling; on the other hand imagination becomes sterile when it remains unfertilized by contact with the objective world. The successful literary artist must derive inspiration from both subjective and objective sources. Thus Blake, the apostle of the imagination, fails most when he loses all contact with life, for imagination itself works best when it has sometimes to come to grips with what is beyond the artist's control; and there is no lack of examples to show how low are the levels to which the sincerest propaganda may sink when it is unrelieved by any felicity of expression. Action and reaction, the more artificial and the less, the mastery of the environment and of the creature, must follow each other in the life of the artist as in the history of art and in the life of every organism. Carlyle exaggerates thus: 'All great Poems, all great Books, if you search the first foundation of their greatness, have been veridical, the truest they could get to be. Never will there be a great Poem more that is not veridical, that does not ground itself on interpreting of Fact; to the rigorous exclusion of all falsity, fiction, idle dross of every kind: never can a Poem truly interest human souls, except by, in the first place, taking with it the *belief* of said souls. Their belief; that is the whole basis, essence, and practical outcome, of human souls: leave that behind you, as 'Poets' everywhere have for a long time done, what is there left the Poets and you.' [11] But the difference is one of approach and not of ultimate aim: Carlyle and Blake and every other real artist

---

[11]   *Latter-Day Pamphlets, The Fine Arts.*

try to arrive at the one truth that informs the Nature without and the Nature within the soul.

Historically, literature has oscillated between realism and romanticism, but the pulse of sculpture and painting is more easily felt. The graphic arts of a young and barbaric civilization are archaic: natural forms are conventionalized; the technique of accurate representation has not yet been mastered. But as skill in delineating natural forms improves, so the contribution of the artist's imagination tends to decline, and the imitation of nature finally achieved is the death of art; such a goal gained is the defeat of the artist and the technician's triumph. The only course is to turn again to the opposite goal, to aim again at expression. And so the pendulum swings. It is interesting to note that the individual recapitulates the history of the race in this sphere as well as in many others. The child begins to draw, not what he sees, but what he thinks he sees; he draws as he imagines, and his work, though not yet art in the full sense, has all the imaginative qualities that the grown artist tries to recapture. The traditional method of training has been to teach the child to suppress his imagination, to draw only what he sees or what he is told to see. So he learns painfully the technique of representation, only to find that he must with even greater difficulty learn to recapture the child's frame of mind, to revive the spontaneity that he has been at such pains to check. And this is no easy task for the intellectual adult.

The history of our Western civilization shows an analogous progress and reversion in art. The collapse of the Roman Empire saw an end of realistic sculpture, which had become almost as lifeless as it was lifelike. Whether the Byzantine and Gothic artists were incapable of producing likenesses, or whether, as Mr. Frank Rutter believes, they chose not to attempt to do so, the fact remains that their sculptures and paintings were decorative and symbolic rather than naturalistic. Then in the fifteenth century came the Renaissance of classic literature, and along with it a revival of the naturalistic ideals of Graeco-Roman art. The science of representation was studied closely, and particularly by the Florentine painters of the fifteenth century. In the hands of the great masters, however, the sciences of chiaroscuro and perspective, though the results of patient attention to nature, were employed to serve the ends of a subtler imaginativeness than appears in some of the cruder distortions. Their followers were less successful, and naturalism culminated in the nineteenth century with the astonishing verisimilitudes of those painters whose aim seems to have been to emulate or to outdo the photographer.

It was the camera as much as anything else which revealed the bankruptcy of academic painting. If imitation of nature were the end of the artist, then the photographer could rival even the man who stuck real feathers onto his canvas to make his still-life more convincing than ever. The time had arrived for a restatement of the aim of art; a reaction was necessary. Curiously enough the reversion was at first towards a new naturalism. The Impressionists tried to obtain a more faithful portrayal of the momentary vision, to substitute for the conventional rendering of a subject the painter's unbiased impression, and above all to imitate the brilliance of natural colouring by applying their pigments in separate spots.

Such, at any rate, were their professed aims; frequently their work was so unlike the impressions of the average man that he regarded the Impressionists with the scorn which he usually reserves for those who depart from Nature. But the Post-Impressionists of every category made no claim to paint as they saw or as anyone could see. The vision of the outward eye merges with the vision of the inward; the painter expresses his feelings about his subject by painting imaginatively, distorting form and colour to do so. And the Cubists took further liberties with nature and eliminated all curves from their paintings. The straight line, they said, is stronger than the curved, and accordingly everything is crystallized into angular, though for the most part still recognizable forms. It was an easy step from the earlier work of Picasso to an art that is almost abstract, where pattern altogether takes the place of imitation and references to nature are obscure or absent. Balls and Kandinsky, and Wyndham Lewis in this country, appear to have arrived at the goal of complete refusal to represent anything but the abstract, towards which the Impressionists set out some fifty years ago. It would not be rash to predict the turn of the pendulum. Undoubtedly imaginative art will require sooner or later the revivifying treatment of external limitations if it is to remain vital.

Such, in barest outline, has been the history of painting in our own civilization. Prof. Flinders Petrie has described no fewer than eight cycles through which the Mediterranean and European peoples have passed. [12] He bases his conclusions in the main upon a study of the

---

12   *Revolutions of Civilization.*

history of sculpture. Each age, Prof. Petrie maintains, has at first an archaic phase, when sculptural representation is crude; there follows a period during which ever greater skill is acquired till almost perfect likenesses are made; a decline then sets in, and is eventually followed by a return to barbarism, which lasts till the cycle begins again.

The most modern and most mechanized methods of visual representation, photography and cinematography, have, during their brief history, been exploited as means of recording and communicating useful information, but they have also provided a new medium of the creative imagination. Successful, if not popular, abstract films have been made, and there is every grade between these and the news-reel, where nevertheless both cutting and point of view offer much scope for imaginative treatment. The cartoon especially, which is really a mode of painting that employs the third dimension of time, has unrivalled possibilities for a man with such a fertile and felicitous inventiveness as Mr. Walt Disney. At the opposite extreme, some of the Soviet propaganda films are supreme examples of artistic excellence combined with utilitarian purpose and sincerity.

So much for action and reaction in the representational arts. Our survey has omitted a vast amount of material that might be brought forward to show how men have swayed from imitation to imagination and back again. But the point has been made clear enough. Let us turn to the arts which remain, to those which do not attempt to copy nature. Obviously they cannot be treated in quite the same way as the imitative arts. But they too have, like any other human activity, their degrees of artificiality; they also range between the more determined and the free.

Let us take, for example, the so-called fine art of architecture. Certainly the architect does not set out to imitate natural forms. Nevertheless the limitations imposed upon him are even stricter than those which apply to the painter who is commissioned to make a portrait. For on every hand the architect has to comply with external requirements, with what is, for him, the nature of things. His walls must be stable; his beams must be proportioned to their loads; the accommodation that he provides must be adequate. In short, he has a programme which must be rigidly observed. Inventiveness he needs, and imagination to find the most fitting solution to his problems, but these truly creative qualities have but a narrow space in which to act: the validity of the designer's inventions must be tested by continual reference to the given conditions. That he shall provide 'commodity and firmness' is the first consideration; the other requisite of architecture, 'delight', may in the designer's opinion have arrived meanwhile unnoticed, as a by-product of efficiency, or it may be thought lacking, in which event some modification or embellishment will be attempted. At this point there is a greater freedom. Ornament, colour, texture—these are matters in which the architect has a little more latitude of operation, though even here the limitations are, as a rule, narrow enough.

Architecture, together with its allied arts and crafts, has in fact a dual nature. It is both an art and an applied science. And its composite structure is reflected in current theories of architectural practice. The most vital movement of our time labels itself 'functionalist', since its supporters hold that a good building—that is, efficient building—is necessarily beautiful, and has no need of artificial aids to make it so. They have reacted against the more human contribution to building; to them the more artificial devices of the drawing-board are unlovely and superfluous. Their revolt, in so far as it has actually taken effect, is essentially a return to nature, or rather to what is nearer to nature. On the other hand we have the extreme traditionalists, who stress the artistic side of architectural practice and are usually prepared to make utility and economy give way here and there to considerations of appearance, while incorporating, if at all possible, the bric-a-brac of long deceased styles. Midway between the functionalists and the traditionalists lie perhaps the majority of the best English architects, who put utility before formal considerations, but employ a modest amount of ornament of a conventional kind.

We may detect a close parallel between the doctrine of Joad and Sinclair [13] with regard to literature, and the doctrine of extreme functionalism in architecture. They agree in this: that beauty is most likely to be won by disregarding its existence, by concentrating upon usefulness rather than by deliberate aestheticism. And their contention is unassailable if by beauty we mean, not beauty in general, but that kind which approaches natural beauty. Of the three kinds of works in which beauty may sometimes be found, namely, the natural, the artificial that has to conform to nature, and free design, the second is taken and the others are left. The functionalists' is a

---

13   See page X.

valuable but partial view. Carried far enough it rules art, in the proper sense, out of court entirely, and leaves only the technician and those who admire his work for the qualities that he has all innocently put into it. But in fact, and fortunately for architecture as an art, the extreme functionalist scarcely ever lives up to his theories. The artist in him is not so easily subdued. Very few purely functional buildings, without so much as one feature or coloured surface or texture that is strictly unnecessary, have been erected by architects professing the creed of extreme utilitarianism. Their training and aesthetic sensibilities war against their intellectual theories. The engineer who has, as a rule, no such bias, is far better able to produce what the functionalist so admires.

But a compromise between the divergent claims of the functionalists and the formalists may easily be found if we delimit the proper sphere of each party. If we distinguish between that kind of structure which must be utilitarian through and through, and that which is not so rigidly determined, between, for example, the power-station and the church, it becomes clear that the former is well within the province of the man with the functionalist approach, while the latter requires the hand of the artist. Both kinds of building of course, need to be designed to give the best possible service, but practical considerations alone will not suffice to make of the church an instrument suited to its function. It must have another kind of utility. It must be psychologically functional. When every practical contingency has been duly allowed for, when every necessity and comfort from acoustics to fonts and footstools has been provided, we are left with little more than a bare shell of a building, suitable enough for a workshop perhaps, but an incongruous setting for traditional worship. It is of vital importance to note that architecture is a far more socialized art than painting or literature. Public taste may be slowly and painfully educated to appreciate the new architecture; meanwhile the architect, to a much greater extent than the practitioner of the other arts, must dance attendance on the public, rather than set out to impose his private tastes whether they prove acceptable or no. If the church fails to conform to and to re-enforce the mood of the worshipper, then it is, strictly speaking, inefficient. However finely regulated the heating and ventilating arrangements, however trim and strong the structure, the whole work is utterly unfunctional, far more so indeed than the coldest and draughtiest and darkest of churches in the familiar styles. And there is another reason why the artist should design churches. Adequate accommodation for a body of worshippers and priests may be provided in a vast number of ways, cost and convenience varying only slightly between them. There are innumerable solutions to the problem before the designer. The programme of the industrial building leaves little room for alternatives; choice, if there is any, lies between the efficient and the slightly less efficient. The designer of the church, on the other hand, has to choose from a large number of equally practical schemes, the form which best expresses the purpose of his building, and to dress this form in such a way as to arouse the appropriate sentiments in his clients.

A graded list of buildings might be made, commencing with those of the factory class, followed by the warehouse, shop, and office types, then by domestic buildings, municipal centres, and places of worship, and concluding with civic monuments. Such a list would commence in the province of the engineer, pass by small gradations to the architect's, and conclude in the sculptor's. At the head of the list would be those structures in which free artificial design is most out of place; at the end would be those where artistic invention is absolutely indispensable. And it would indicate to what degree the architect must adopt the role of engineer on the one hand, and the role of artist on the other. Many deplorable blunders would be avoided if the distinction between efficient beauty and artistic beauty were fully realized by designers, and the proper field of each were clearly defined.

The recent reversion towards unrelieved functionalism is probably a far more complete denial of the place of art in architecture than has ever occurred before. Nevertheless it is possible to trace, in almost every historical style, an initial period of structural experiment, culminating in the heyday of achievement. The technical problems have been solved by the adaptation of the form to its environment, to the world beyond the designer's control. As yet the bare bones of the building are not over-encumbered with ornament; but soon a time of ripe accomplishment arrives which ends in *tours de force* and artificial elaborations. In the history of architecture as in the history of painting, there is always a movement either towards imaginative unrestricted expression or towards a rigorous conformity to what is given, to the nature and the natural laws that lie beyond the world of the artist's proper activity.

We have devoted a somewhat disproportionate space to architecture because buildings are typical of a host of artefacts that come partly within the range of the practical craftsman, and partly within the range of the artist. Instead of architecture we might have taken the art of costume, of furniture design or town planning to illustrate what is true of all the semi-practical and semi-artistic pursuits of man. What has been said of architecture applies, *mutatis mutandis,* to all the rest in a large degree. The swing of our pendulum is to be detected here no less than in the arts of representation. From time to time there arise those who would free the useful instrument of many of its useless trappings, who would rid architecture of constructed ornament, clothes of their more fantastic extravagances, furniture of its knobs and claws and carvings, pottery of its garlands of roses, and so forth. Then, when these reformers have had their day, there arise others who reassert the right of the imagination to make of any useful object whatsoever a vehicle of its more artificial creations. Ornament of another kind goes back to the building; clothes again become luxurious and a burden; knobs and claws and garlands are again to be seen about the house; though of other patterns and applications. At length men tire again of the artificial, and revert to the kind of beauty that only rigid subservience to what is given and immutable can provide.

Before we turn to the purest, the most abstract of all the arts, to wit, music, let us remind ourselves of one of the conclusions at which we arrived in our first chapter. We saw that nature, in one of its aspects, embraced all well-established human traditions, all the accomplished work of man that cannot be changed because it lies in the past. This also is for the artist something that is given; it is part of the world beyond his control. *Any* departure from tradition then, even if it is a reversion from the ornate to the simple, from the formal to the functional, is at the time of its departure seen as artificial. It is a revolt from what is to what shall be; therefore it is creative and artificial in one sense, though it may be a turning again towards nature in another sense. On the other hand, the revival of past forms, the repetition of what has already been effected, is a swinging of the pendulum towards nature and away from artifice. The motion of the pendulum is relative to our point of view. If we choose to regard a particular art as an activity of our species in its relations with an outside world, (as so far we have done) then we conclude that the pendulum swings towards that outside world when the artist's work is determined by exterior conditions, and away from it when his work is free from such domination. But if instead we regard the artist as an individual in relation to his artistic predecessors and contemporaries, then whenever he departs from tradition, whenever he produces *original* work, such work is artificial, and whenever he imitates, whenever his work is derivative, the pendulum has turned again towards nature.

Music is one of the most subjective and artificial of human creations. There can be no question here of imitating nature or of practical utility. It is the unique status of music among the arts that it does not continually shift away from or towards conformity with the outside world. It remains unconcerned with what is beyond itself. But *within* itself there is a continual motion either towards a tradition that has become as nature or towards the new and the artificial. Yet even for the composer there is somewhat given besides the works of the past. Nature the unchangeable consists for him of the laws of harmony and dissonance, the gamut and tone of the instruments at his disposal, and the limitations of the human interpreter.

I have stressed the artificiality of art. It is now necessary to qualify this emphasis. Art is born in the unconscious. What proceeds from the lower strata of the artist's mind is outside his conscious control. Certainly deep instincts may be repressed and a conscious direction may be given to the imagination, but exactly what we shall imagine and how we shall feel are beyond all conscious determination. The painter, if he is a great one, paints largely as he must; the musician must write down the tunes that ring in his head or steal what he cannot imagine. The artist is free, but free only to achieve self-expression, to be himself. This is the only ultimate meaning which can be attached to freedom: the capacity and opportunity to give vent to one's own nature. Outside lies an uncontrolled world; within lies another uncontrollable world. The action of the latter upon the former is what we know as artifice; at the point of friction between these two worlds there is what we know as freedom. In so far as a man retires into himself and ignores the outer world, he has turned from Nature and artifice, to his own nature. And this nature of his, because it is grounded in the common Nature which underlies all things, is capable of taking him to the very heart of existence.

Such, at least, is the mystic's claim. An abandonment of appearances and a retirement into the recesses of one's own nature; not a mere revelling in an imaginary world more to one's taste than the real one, but an arduous search for the inmost reality that is normally obscured by the senses: these are the hall-marks of mysticism. By such means the great contemplatives profess to gain those experiences of reality that cannot be conveyed by language. The scientist seeks truth in nature, the mystic in the depths of his own being. Their approach differs, and their aims are by no means exactly coincident, but they have this in common, that they are naturalists.

Art is never quite devoid of mystical content. The distortions of the painter's canvas and the poet's license would be no more than futile mannerisms if they were not used to probe beneath the sensuous fact. Art is an active and often unconscious kind of mysticism; failing to be so it is no longer art in the narrower sense. The artist departs from the immediate truth to tell a deeper one. Carlyle said of Shakespeare's art: 'Such a man's works, whatsoever he with utmost conscious exertion and forethought shall accomplish, grow up withal _un_consciously, from the unknown deeps in him; as the oak-tree grows from the Earth's bosom, as the mountains shape themselves with a symmetry grounded on Nature's own laws, conformable to all Truth whatsoever.' 14

14   _Heroes and Hero-worship_

Our extremes, then, have met. The artificial pushed far enough completes the circle and becomes nature. Search outside yourself and you will come upon the unknown and will suspect the unknowable. Search patiently within and you will come upon the same abyss. It is as inevitable that the most profound philosophers and scientists should, by thrusting deep into nature, wander into mysticism, as that the creative artist, by travelling in the opposite direction, should verge upon the same territory. All roads, if we do not lose ourselves in side-tracks, lead eventually to the seldom glimpsed battlements of eternity.

CHAPTER VIII

The Future of the Artificial

Whither does artifice lead? Is industrialism about to herald a new age of prosperity, leisure and cultural advancement? Does technical progress ensure progressive human welfare, till we are all landed safely in a golden age? Few are now so confident. Even the incurable optimists have ceased to regard progress, in any way that matters, as quite inevitable. And the most mournful pessimist has more than enough evidence to lend speciousness to his lamentations. But the fate of our own Western civilization and the destiny of the whole species, are matters beyond the prophetic power of the author and the size of this book to encompass. Whether civilization is to perish by means of its own horrible engines of slaughter, whether new conquests, with new eras of barbarism and racial intermixture, will bring our age to a close and see the commencement of another, whether the zenith of our race is passed and all that remains is a slow degeneration, or whether, by luck or good management, we shall survive all our troubles—these problems are indeterminate till man shall supply his own answer. The end of all, however, seems inescapable. Unless humanity can find another home in the universe, or dispense with corporeal life altogether, the cooling down of the earth and the solar system is likely to kill all terrestrial organisms. Even if an entirely new kind of organism were evolved, that would be adapted to another order of conditions than ours, there remains the fact, or rather the theory, that the universe as a whole is running down. But even this is not absolutely final. If the doctrine of Entropy does not soon meet with the same doom as that which it prescribes for the universe, but does indeed correspond with fact, who will venture to say that what is running down shall never be rewound, that what has by some unfathomable agency been energized, shall not by the same agent be energized again?

But these are hidden matters. The probable future of the artificial works of man remains our problem—their future, that is, if the present tendencies are developed further by our own culture or one that is to follow. We commence with the hypothesis that artifice has not yet reached its peak, that Life has not by any means finished with her latest and oddest experiment. We are making, of course, a mere supposition, and many would describe this progress of artifice as, in reality, a steep decline, if indeed it ever happens. This question too, whether technical advancement is or is not in the best interests of man, would require several volumes to do it justice, and as far as possible we shall avoid pronouncing a verdict upon it. Our aim is simply to try to infer from what has been discussed in the earlier chapters, namely, the past and present of the artificial, its future trend, to plot a little further the curves which have already been traced. In such speculation there can of course be nothing more than a statement of my opinion and some restatements of the opinions of our amateur and professional prophets.

The astounding development of machines in the nineteenth century cannot fail to suggest the course of their further evolution. It is likely to be a progress in many directions, where new species are continually branching from the parent stem, where novel environments are continually being created by some machines and producing corresponding adaptations in others. For mechanical devices are like organisms in this respect, that they form together a close-knit association—even a kind of unit—in which the destinies of many are interlocked, and change anywhere has repercussions where they are least to be expected. Machines, while they become specialized along many divergent lines, yet move in concert.

There is bound, for example, to be an advance in automatism among many very different kinds of devices. Machines will become far more sensitive to varying degrees of the same kind of stimulus and to a greater variety of stimuli. Their 'sense organs' will become more refined and more discriminating. Already, as we have seen, man has supplemented his own meagre set of senses by employing those of animals and by using mechanical detectors. Thermometers and barometers, the mariner's compass, the balance and the measuring rod, the micrometer and the clock, are a few among the more familiar of the instruments with which we have made some of our sense impressions more reliable, and made good the lack of others. But nothing could be more certain than that we have only begun to appreciate the powers of the machine in this field. The complexity of the organism is its chief shortcoming so far as the accurate registration of external conditions is concerned: because each has his unique history, no two men will make an exactly equal estimation of the same external condition, unless they are provided with artificial aids. Every experience of ours is tinged with the colour of a thousand others. It is often as much a reflection of ourselves as of the external event. It is impure and, for science, unreliable. Only by the assistance of simpler mechanisms than those we were born with can we begin to understand nature or to control it. Experimental science needs these artificial organs to detect and to measure; applied science needs them to effect changes. In the former case it is the human body that is supplied with the additional organs; in the latter it is rather the machine which is endowed with the means of registering the significant characters of its environment and of reacting accordingly.

Machines are rapidly becoming more sensitive. The slightest change in temperature, in the intensity of light, in colour, as well as in velocity and direction, can be recorded by instruments that have already been invented. Mechanisms are made that respond to a note of a given pitch, and there are many automatic devices for detecting differences and likenesses of shape, density and weight. And once an accurate registration of some influence can be obtained, it is usually possible to connect the artificial sense organ to a contrivance that will provide automatically the required response. Thus the typical automaton is constructed after the manner of the organism, with three kinds of parts: first the measuring instrument or detector, such as the magnetic compass or the thermostat; this is connected to a second device for estimating from the findings of the 'sense organs' what adjustment shall be made by the third part. A simple illustration is the automatic electric pump, where a float in the storage tank operates a switch as soon as the water has reached a certain low level; thereupon the pump is set in motion till the float is raised again to a predetermined high level, when the switch is turned, the electric circuit is broken, and the pump ceases to work. Here the means of measurement is provided by the material to be measured; the part that corresponds to the brain comprises the float and the switch, and the 'limbs' consist of the motor, the pump and the service pipe. By means of this simple contrivance a constant supply of water may be maintained for years with scarcely any human attention.

In the course of two or three generations many far more ingenious automata than this one have been made. What might a thousand years of steady development in this direction not bring forth? At the moment there lies in the path one great difficulty—the automaton responds only to a definite, clearly delimited condition; so far it is largely incapable of 'generalizing', of recognizing similarities between a number of objects of which none is exactly like any other, of detecting, for example, among a variety of bodies, those that are more or less cylindrical in shape though of different sizes and proportions. It lacks a faculty corresponding to the human faculty of forming universal conceptions, which permits the recognition of objects as the same in the midst of change. To a cylinder of specified dimensions, placed in a specified position, the mechanical eye can be made to respond, but to recognize the shape, of whatever material, size or proportions, is beyond the automaton's power. But difficulties almost as formidable as those which confront us here have been overcome in the history of invention, and it is safe to say that machines will become far more self-sufficient and far less dependent upon the human factor that is in many ways so ill-adjusted to the business of machine-minding.

But there is a depressing alternative, with which Mr. H. G. Wells and Mr. Aldous Huxley have made us familiar. The worker who is now so temperamental, so often conscious that his faculties are worthy of higher tasks than those his routine can offer, whose interests are so often outside his work, may, by judicious selection, be made into a docile creature, adapted wholly to industrial conditions, rendered harmless and efficient by the loss of all that lifts him above the condition of a mere tool. The problem must soon arise, indeed it has already arisen—shall our automata come of human or of machine stock? Human life is notoriously cheap and delicate machines costly, and our captains of industry are more concerned with present profits than with prophets of the future. But the workers themselves may have something to say upon the question, and radical changes in our economic system may render the differentiation of society into rigid castes an improbable development. And there is the further fact that as the productivity of machines increases and they regulate themselves more and more, so the length of time which must be spent upon their attendance is progressively reduced, provided, of course, that the demand for luxuries is not allowed to keep pace with production. At any rate there are considerable grounds for the belief that all, or nearly all, drudgery will be imposed upon the machine, that all mere routine work and much labour that is complex but uninteresting will be transferred from a human proletariat to a mechanical one. There would remain, of course, certain contingencies, as breakdowns so serious that they could not be dealt with by the machine itself, and the recent discoveries and inventions would entail a good deal of work at the time of their incorporation. *But the very qualities which render work unsuitable for an automaton are those which make it a more fit and engrossing work for a man.*

A nearly manless industry, a strange, utterly unhuman world, full of monsters incredibly powerful, yet sensitive to influences that no organism has ever noticed; a world of minute and gigantic creatures, some of them hinting by fantastic eyes and arms and fingers at the tiny god that made them; a mechanical society that is a whole, where intimate links bind every member visibly and invisibly into one Mechanism, whose sole end and beginning is Man—somewhat thus might we picture the industry of the future. The leisure that was once the prerogative of the elite is now available for all. Time and enough to spare now for pure science, for art, and the essentials of civilization. The effect of such leisure will depend upon the kind of man to whom it is given. Such a new age will need a new man. But more of him later; machines concern us now.

The mean chip of rock and the broken bough that our forefather enterprisingly added to his body have grown and grown beyond belief. The first has proved a very Moses' rock for abundance, the second a very Aaron's rod for fertility. From a small grasped thing without the slightest power to shift for itself, a rude insensitive object that owes all its importance in our eyes to him who deigned to hold it for a moment—from such humble stock has the great artificial race sprung. Its growth to any outside observer must be as astonishing as the growth of the tree of life itself, of which the artificial is a kind of bastard branch born of an irregular union of life with matter. The inert tool grows in bulk till it becomes immovable and a thousand times greater than its master; it becomes organized till it leaps into activity of its own making. One unwelcome caress from his tool will send a man to his long home. It has faculties that no man ever had. Though far inferior to the creature in many respects, Life has achieved by its means what was impossible with protoplasm. Yet, for all their increasing self-sufficiency, machines are still the supplements of flesh and bone; their *raison d'être* is the individual that they prolong. Their growth is his.

New materials and new methods are bound to have an incalculable influence over man's destiny. We rely at present for our industrial materials largely upon the mineral and organic substances with which nature is pleased to provide us. Some of these are refined and built up to suit our requirements, but our methods are crude compared with the methods of Life. But as the properties of organized matter come to be better understood, the machine may be made to imitate in some ways the constitution of the organism, while still retaining those characters which render it more efficient than the living creature. About the intimate processes of the organism so little is at present known that it is impossible to guess how physiology may give hints to technology, and in the meantime there is much difficult work to be done.

To render themselves virtually independent of the rest of organisms will be one of the tasks of our descendants. To synthesise foodstuffs from inorganic matter, to become, in effect and by means of artificial extensions, *plants,* would be a great stride forward in the direction of man's material emancipation. Man is a parasite upon vegetables, which alone among organisms possess the secret of building edible substances from the inorganic. There is a fair promise that man will regain this primitive faculty and become by artifice a 'vegetable' once more.

A part of our prophecy that will probably be sooner realized is concerned with harnessing the forces of nature. Many of our methods are now extraordinarily crude. Hand power, animal power, and coal power that imposes such hard conditions upon so many, must before long be replaced by more scientific appropriations of force. There exist practically inexhaustible sources of energy in wind, tides, the molten interior of the earth, sunlight, and matter itself. Once economical means of exploiting these vast reservoirs have been found, there remains no reason why the energy which invigorates the greater body of man should not become almost entirely independent of the metabolic energy at the centre. These new resources at man's command, the artificializing of the planet may proceed rapidly. We content ourselves now with a sporadic interference with the character of our terrestrial home. Its configuration we accept, and make the best of it. But the earth was not planned in advance as a human habitation; it must be made into such. If darkness lasts too long, if temperature is not to our liking, if mountains and valleys and rivers impede the human plan, then these shall be made to conform to human convenience. The means will be ready to hand. The earth itself will be caught up in the wheels of human evolution; the hitherto ungovernable will become plastic in the hands of its new master. No longer will man adapt himself respectfully to the caprices of the earth's crust; the once formidable obstacle will be adapted to himself and to the instruments of his life. But always it is a question of degree. Man will never put all things under his feet, and even the earth will continue to defy him till the end. And, of course, we must always remember that the effect which he is likely to exert upon the universe is almost negligible.

But this insignificant fragment of the world he has some chance of making his own. The earth and Man may become almost synonymous terms. The earth tends to become the 'body' of society, a great 'organism' hurtling through space, its character as a whole only fully appreciable to an outside observer. Today a machine is planned and a building is designed before the first brick is laid. Tomorrow the method will be extended to our cities, and eventually to the inter-urban spaces and the entire surface of the globe. Not only will the earth become more and more the body of Man, but it will become increasingly a designed, an artificial corpus.

The idea of the plan, though it lies at the root of intelligence, has been slow to spread to the larger social activities of man. It has flourished again and again and been swallowed up in chaos, only to be revived with new vigour. This is nowhere better seen than in the art of town-planning. The Romans, and before them the Babylonians, knew well how to lay out an orderly arrangement of streets, and almost all of the longer roads in this country that are not dangerously and absurdly tortuous we owe to the thoroughness of the Roman engineer. Paris, says M. Le Corbusier, was designed by an ass, and certainly most towns might well have been devised by some such creature. For in fact they were not planned. For the most part they grew up along the tracks trodden out by beast or man, tracks which turned to avoid a pond here and a hillock there, which meandered towards some objective or none. These trodden ways are now often the great thoroughfares of our cities. Every cable, tube railway, pavement and building line follows sheep-wise the arbitrary wanderings of the first inhabitants. A Methusalah would be able to trace with amused contempt the palimpsests of old trees and field boundaries of his youth, to which the rich city still configures its towers and tunnels. Of course it is true that the plan of the old village was sufficiently adapted to the requirements of that time; the arrangement of its streets, though arbitrary, did not seriously incommode the inhabitant. But to the new conditions the old network is altogether unsuited. But this is not all. Not only have our cities no plans worthy of the name, but their streets, in all but a few cases, have no elevations. Each is for the most part a jumble of uncoordinated enterprises, a fortuitous growth, where houses jostle factories and shops in the general struggle, like plants in the jungle, for light and air; where the endeavour of every shopkeeper is to outdo the startling effect of his neighbour's façade, till the wise tradesman gains your ear by a quiet elevation amid a pandemonium of violent cacophonies. Well-intentioned attempts to mitigate some of the nuisances of our towns have been made in the shape of the Town Planning Acts and various building by-laws, but while the wide limits laid down, and while huge sums are paid to the private owners of property that is appropriated for public purposes, so long will our towns remain a discredit to the human intelligence, intolerable to any self-respecting ancient Roman, and anomalies in an age of electric grids and airways. Someone has suggested that a few Roman chariots in the Strand would be more in keeping with the character of that thoroughfare than the stream of highly efficient omnibuses which may now be seen flowing or stagnant there—a quite unmerited slight upon the Roman mind and the Roman town. In point of plan, London, like most towns, is no fit residence for an animal who styles himself intelligent.

All this lack of order is sometimes picturesque enough; but it belongs to nature rather than to man. Untamed landscapes have no straight lines or regular curves save the marine horizon. Then man comes with his measure and imposes geometric forms, drives rectilinear ways in spite of every impediment, impresses upon the earth's surface the ordered patterns that are the symbols of his intelligence, the material counterpart of his steady purpose. In details our cities are highly artificial, in general plan most of them are still deeply infected with nature. In the countryside, nature and artifice are still struggling for dominance, and upon all major issues nature has its way. We lack neither the means nor the knowledge to artificialize town and country, but we lack the necessary form of social organization. Whatever the merits of our present system—

or rather lack of system—compared with a planned economy, this much is certain—that because we are permitted so much individual planning there is no general plan; that if a tithe of the effort and ability now spent in enterprises which conflict and so neutralize one another, were spent in laying down a general scheme, within which the schemes of the individual had yet much free play, then our towns and cities, our economic and political organizations, would take on a more rational pattern. Waste and wear would be reduced beyond belief. The care and thought that is now lavished upon the design of a single machine or building would be extended to the design of the new town and the gradual refashioning of old ones.

Many will object that the regimentation of the individual has gone quite far enough. Possibly so, but very probably it will go much further. We are not concerned here with the desirability of such developments, but only with their possibility. And before hastily condemning the restriction of liberty, we might well ask ourselves the questions—whether some kinds of liberty do not in the long run defeat their own purpose, and whether it is not sometimes necessary to prescribe a bondage that leads to a fuller freedom. But liberty is a most ambiguous term, capable of many interpretations. Whatever happens, its meanings for governors and governed are bound to change.

Back of men's attitude to social systems lies the fact that they have scarcely done more than feel about such matters and only occasionally have begun to think about them. The hand has been the schoolmaster of the intelligence. Tools, things handled, things out of which tools might possibly be fashioned, are the objects about which intelligence has been built up. This part of the world, the part out of which instruments are made, has been thoroughly secularized. Reason is here in its own familiar field; here is no place for dogmatic assertion and denial, but for patient experiment. There are no wars, no fiery speeches and campaigns of agitation to contest the superiority of one tool over another, to uphold the merits, for example, of travel by rail as compared with travel by road. Both are tested and tried. Man is here a reasonable animal, anxious to examine the facts and to profit by his own and other's experience. Tell him that one tool is better than another, and he will listen with interest and go about to discover if it be so. But tell the same man that communism is preferable to capitalism, or *vice versa*, and he will find it difficult to control himself. Very rarely will he consider carefully the evidence for both sides before arriving at a conclusion. This heat, this emotion and unreason, show that we are leaving the field of artifice and approaching nature, the sphere where man is not yet master. The structure of society has grown, not arbitrarily, and not according to the deliberate intention of men, but in accordance with its own natural laws of development. But these laws admit of many changes, and man may think it desirable to alter in some respects the ground-plan of the whole structure. Long tradition has given institutions the attribute of naturalness; they remain hallowed till some iconoclast proclaims his challenge. Ever since Plato wrote his *Republic* there have been forthcoming plans for the artificial, the deliberately devised forms of social organization, and some scattered attempts to found communities anew, on preconceived principles. The prophets and thinkers, helped by the difficulties in which the natural society finds itself from time to time, are beginning to gain a hearing. What passed for inviolable and immutable nature is already staked out by artifice. By disasters and avoidable suffering men are being driven to take up their claim. Even that familiar expression of the economist, *laisser faire,* implies the new frame of mind, and suggests that the system in question is permitted to remain on sufferance only, till we shall choose to change it.

The leaven of intelligence is beginning to work and spread itself within the greater body of the individual. There are unmistakable signs that the proper sphere of reason is extending outwards from a man's tools to his larger social constitution, and inwards, to the living core. 'We are fearfully and wonderfully made,' says the old writer, as though to warn us that we are again on holy ground. We are made in the image of God, believed our fathers, and Moses alone was permitted a glimpse of His back parts. Government and medicine, that is to say, the ordering of the social and the individual body, have from very early times been inextricably mixed with religious practices; thus kings were either divine in their own right or divinely appointed, and even the priests of Esculapius sought to cure by purely religious exercises. Similar notions survive today; but both the body politic and the body individual are the subjects of patient research, and to discover what exists is the first step towards intelligent control. The whole of Man, from gametes to distribution of wealth, comes eventually under the critical purview of intelligence.

Biological invention is bound to meet with far more resistance than mechanical invention. Changes in the fleshly body will have to be introduced very gradually, and it is not unlikely that serious clashes will occur between the defenders of the *status quo* and the innovators. Anything unfamiliar will certainly be called a perversion until it has become a commonplace, when it will be taken for nature.

Little need be said about the science of eugenics. Many do not doubt that the time has arrived when at least some of the recommendations of eugenicists should be legally enforced. It is a matter of the greatest urgency that our least desirable citizens should be prevented from transmitting hereditary diseases and feeble-mindedness to the next generation. But this task once begun, more positive and ambitious schemes are likely to be set on foot. Man has moulded his domestic animals and plants to his requirements. Because of the greater risk, because of the lack of certain knowledge, and because of prejudice, he has not begun to build the kind of body that he desires for himself. Perhaps he does not yet know what he wants, save that he dislikes certain diseases. But once having undertaken the correction of the worst and most obvious evils, the way for more constructive measures has been opened out. We cannot see very far ahead with any distinctness but the immediate goal is clearly visible. When that has been gained then a new goal will appear, new deficiencies will be found in what before passed for perfect, and new crusades will be started. So, by easy stages, probably without any clear sense of their direction, men will alter their organic constitution. They will substitute for the more arbitrary processes of natural selection a planned artificial selection. Humane customs in society have already interfered with the salutary effects of the former to such an extent that the only ways by which degeneration may be avoided are either to revert to savagery or to take the opposite road, the way of artifice. The middle path, lying half-way between the natural and the artificial, leads only to destruction.

The practice of eugenics is an indirect method of determining the future of the organism. There is a second means to the same end, a more direct road, that does not take the place of the first, yet leads as inevitably to a new kind of body for man. The tool which began as an external appendage is beginning to penetrate the body. We noticed in an earlier chapter that the work of replacing the natural organs by artificial substitutes was commenced long ago. The flesh is not safe against the onslaughts of intelligence. The eugenicist accepts the living tissue he desires to change, but the orthopaedist and the dentist introduce the inanimate organ when the live one proves inadequate. More significant than their merely palliative devices are those used in contraception. Here we have a most important new faculty added. Again plan is substituted for chance. Nature has ordained that procreation shall as a rule attend sexual pleasure, but man has ordained that he shall be exempted from this rule. He has asserted his independence, and, what is more important for us here, commenced to meddle with the flesh, by direct means to give it new powers. The surgeons' aim is as a rule curative; he attempts to restore normal functioning, not to add super-normal powers. But sometimes he has recourse to artificial aids of the flesh, and always he manipulates the living tissue, working upon it with knives and saws and needles like any joiner or sempstress upon wood or fabric. The human body is a machine bequeathed to us by our fathers; we receive it as a gift from the past as we receive the locomotive and the dynamo. Like them it has reached a certain stage in its evolution, and like any other machine it is capable of being improved. It does not now differ in any important respect from the human body of twenty centuries ago, except that its environment has changed utterly. It is, in many ways, ill adapted to the extensions that envelop it, but it has begun to progress or degenerate (the two terms are almost interchangeable, being but different views of the same process) by the same means that have determined also the evolution of its outer instruments, by the intelligence that resides within it.

Prof. J. B. S. Haldane has suggested that by the middle of the present century scientists will have produced the first ectogenetic child, that is to say, a human embryo will have been reared to maturity outside the mother's body. He believes, in effect, that man will become oviparous, will revert to a condition analogous with that of the reptilian stock from which he has sprung. Maternity for a highly civilized woman is a dangerous and difficult business, and may become more so. There are signs that one day man will cease to be a viviparous animal whose offspring are, for the first few months of life, parasites upon their mothers. The artificial egg, consisting perhaps of a glass bottle containing the growing embryo and an enveloping serum, will relive the mother of most of the inconveniences of child-bearing. Doubtless she will lose in some ways by the change, but it is inevitable that every advance shall be attended by some retrogression. Very possibly the mothers of the future will sometimes look back with regret to the good old times of pregnancy and obstetrics, but it is more likely that, given a sufficient lapse of time, they will learn with surprise of the dark days of pain and disfigurement, and congratulate themselves upon their superior civilization, their more enlightened naturalness. Nowadays, of course, perhaps the majority of mothers would regard ectogenesis as a shocking perversion, an ingenious and revolting piece of devilment.

If there could be any doubt that artifice is nothing more nor less than Life working through her most illustrious child, performing through him what she could not otherwise achieve, we do not lack indications that man's efforts are of a piece with Life's. Man, while groping forward slowly and almost blindfold, is surely taking a circular, or rather a spiral course. Progress consists largely of reversion to earlier types, a repetition upon other planes of what has gone before. There arrive many new things under the sun, but each of them reflects an old one while it remains essentially different. Solomon saw the spiral orbit from above and said that there is nothing new; others have caught a side glimpse of it and announced that the old order changes, yielding place to new. The two views are complementary half-truths.

Of the forecasts of things to come that have come to my notice, by far the boldest and most exciting is Mr. J. H. Bernal's *The World, the Flesh and the Devil,* in which he draws a vivid picture of the human body of the future. The limbs so necessary to the savage have become mere parasites upon the body of the civilized man. For many purposes their place has been taken by more efficient artificial organs. A complicated surgical operation is therefore performed upon the man who wishes to abandon the more normal way of life; many of his organs are removed, and replaced where necessary by instruments that make little or no demand upon the tissues that remain. Eventually, only certain irreplaceable parts remain, such as the brain and the organs of sense. Blood is manufactured on a large scale and supplied to the disembodied brains, a number of which share the artificial heart. But the brain is of course only the centre of a vast artificial body. It is one of the last outposts of nature in the entire human organization, controlling artificial organs in every place. The man is physically ill-defined, merging with others like himself, but in mind he remains an individual. Even with such a picture Mr. Bernal is not content. His final view is of a host of entirely artificial beings, like a swarm of clockwork bees, inhabiting the interior of large globes which they navigate through space.

Such a picture may seem of course, utterly fantastic and perhaps revolting. But if we bear in mind the difference between what man is now and what he was, or rather what his ancestors were, a score of millions of years ago, and remember too the swiftness of artificial evolution compared with the natural, then Mr Bernal's account of the artificial man does not appear so wildly improbable as it appears at first, though it may still seem exceedingly unpleasant. His picture is no more than a projection of our present tendencies into the future.

And it would certainly seem that the race's only hope of immortality depends upon whether it is capable of the kind of interstellar navigation that Mr. Bernal has described.

There remain at least two other means by which man may possibly influence the course of his own evolution. At present we have little reliable knowledge concerning telepathy and the psychic phenomena associated with it. There seems to be little reasonable doubt, however, that between some minds, and under certain conditions, communication takes place without the aid of any sensual apparatus. Whether as a race we are slowly acquiring the faculties of telepathy and clairvoyance, or are losing them, may perhaps be a doubtful question. But however that may be, the fact remains that we are gradually learning more about psychic manifestations; a few scientific men are beginning to examine them impartially, without irrational prejudice in any direction. It is just possible that the faculties of telepathy and clairvoyance, if we come to understand them better and possibly to cultivate them in ourselves, may render artificial means of communication unnecessary. Brains would be able to commune with one another and the rest of the world in a direct manner, though it would still be necessary to have organs for effecting material changes. But the superstition which labels as 'hocus pocus' all the facts which do not fit into its framework, and the superstition which, in all simplicity, believes all that it is told—the stranger the story the more implicit the faith—both surround and obscure the evidence for psychic phenomena and make prediction difficult.

Nowadays we hear a good deal about the power of the mind over the body. Most medical men cautiously admit that a patient's condition may be affected adversely or otherwise by his state of mind, but they are generally opposed to any more comprehensive theory. But a number of religious sects and cults go much further and claim that persons with diseases of long standing, whom eminent physicians have failed to cure, and even cases that have been pronounced hopeless, have been cured by mental influence. Sometimes these alleged cures have been ascribed to divine agencies, sometimes to 'the power of the mind to objectify its own beliefs', and sometimes to faith in the efficacy of a person or a specific. However contemptuous some may be regarding the multiform theories and alleged results of the mind-cure cults, 'the plain fact remains', Prof. William James pointed out, 'that the spread of the movement has been due to practical fruits... It is evidently bound to develop still farther, both speculatively and practically... It matters nothing that, just as there are hosts of persons who cannot pray, so there are greater hosts who cannot by any possibility be influenced by the mind-curers' ideas. For our immediate purpose, the important point is that so large a number exist who can be so influenced.' [1] But such power of mind over body once demonstrated, it does not seem improbable that more positive results may be attainable. Mr. Bernard Shaw has told us of future men who will be able to grow any number of heads and limbs by merely desiring them. And a certain type of American author, apparently under the influence of Berkeleyan idealism in a distorted

---

[1]   *The Varieties of Religious Experience*, p.96.

form, sticks at nothing and talks, without apology or qualification, of 'growing the kind of environment you desire by visualizing it.' This may appear far too absurd to admit of consideration, but we may remind ourselves of the words of the teacher who is, in the western hemisphere, considered to be of all authorities the most orthodox, 'If ye have faith as a grain of mustard seed, ye shall say unto this mountain, Remove hence unto yonder place; and it shall remove; and nothing shall be impossible unto you.' But, of course, this is described as a mere parable, and the mountain is supposed to represent some spiritual or mental obstruction. It is, however, our way with the writings of great teachers and reformers to interpret their words at their face value or otherwise as it suits our convenience.

We have ventured upon much doubtful territory, more by way of suggesting some of the myriad possibilities than with the purpose of prediction. One thing remains sufficiently clear—the general direction of man's further evolution. It will be artificial. Man will change often and drastically, and his metamorphoses will be more and more of his own determination. Spite of his conservatism he will leave no accessible particle of himself and his world unexamined. His mind and his body will come under the searchlight of intelligence, and these having become partially illuminated, he is bound to detect from time to time the presence of undesirable characters which must be altered. But the brighter the light the darker the shadows. The deep recesses of nature appear all the deeper as he probes and changes. The more territory artifice claims from nature, the more extensive does nature appear. To the extent that man becomes acquainted with his own nature and modifies it, by so much are the profounder mysteries of his being revealed as utterly beyond the scope of reason and finally unconquerable. Only to complacent ignorance is life crystal-clear.

CHAPTER IX

The Effects of the Instrument upon its User

We have traced in some details the use which living creatures have made of instruments of many kinds. What, in general, are the effects of tool-using upon the organism? Clearly they are very different in different cases. Some tool-users seem to have suffered great loss, others appear to have gained in power and complexity, and occasionally we may hesitate to pronounce upon the character of the effect. There can be no doubt as to the importance of the question before us: to what extent and under what conditions does the artificial or the external instrument lead to the loss of the organism's faculties and organs on one hand, and to the improvement of these on the other hand. Or, to bring the question nearer home; how have men prospered, and how lost, by artifice? If we can supply some more or less satisfactory answers to such questions our enquiry will not have been made in vain.

First let us remember that, though we necessarily distinguish between the organism and its world, the distinction is not between two independent things. Environment and organism are interactive; they are intimately related and mutually dependent. Environment is essential to life, and affected by every vital activity. Environment is the necessary background which defines the creature and is at the same

235

time defined by it. And adaptation, the fitting together of organism and environment, is characteristic of all life whatsoever. There can be no question of improvement here; living things do not become more and more adapted in the course of evolution. Every species of animal and plant is furnished with a sufficiency of tools, for no creature can live without adequate means of life, without instruments that work. The lowliest is as well provided for as the highest, for both live, and to live is evidence of tool-functioning.

Progress consists, not in adaptation to environment, nor in the attainment of independence of the world—if that were possible, but in exercising ever greater control over external conditions. It consists, not in the perfecting of instruments that lie outside the body, but in an extension of the organism's dominion over them so that even the outer environment shall be made serviceable. Some control, some choice, is necessary even when there is no need for the organism to roam in search of a livelihood. The plant, whose exterior instruments are at hand and require no discovery or manipulation, selects from what is given; it takes as much from the earth and the air as it needs and turns its leaves towards the sun. Sessile creatures have a certain power of selection amongst the influences that come their way. But the mobile organism, by changing its world frequently and drastically, does a good deal towards creating and controlling its environment. Where there is choice among many alternatives, there also are relative freedom and independence; where there are many possible adjustments to conditions there arises increased individuality.

The creature whose environment is quite beyond its control,

whose external means of life need little selection and no supervision, has a set of outside instruments that is almost perfect. There are here few faults which must at all costs be made good; the system of tools maintains itself constantly in working order so long as the organism lives. So the plants have neither to toil nor to spin. As fortunate users of tools more adequate than the animals', little is required of the users. These tools, however, are expensive. First, the sessile organism, because its capability of adjustment is so limited, is subject to many accidents. A defect in the instruments of life leads to death unless a new and better instrument can be found or made. If the plant lacks nourishment or shelter, it is unable to seek out a more favourable position and dies; if the seed falls on stony ground it perishes. [1] And second, the adequacy (apart from such accidents) of the tools of the sessile organism is a barrier to any progress of bodily faculties and organs. The various constituents of earth and air of which the plant has need do not have to be chased and fought and killed before they can be of use. Elaborate sense organs and locomotor apparatus are unnecessary to the plant, but to the animal that must search for new grazing grounds and to the predator who must overcome formidable obstacles before his meal is ready for him, such bodily instruments are indispensable.

The mobile animals have, in fact, appropriated a less efficient set of external tools than the plants'. Their more complex structure and behaviour are necessary in order to balance the deficiencies of their

---

1   There is no lack of adaptation here, of course. Organisms with a high death rate must have a correspondingly high birth rate by way of compensation.

exterior instruments. [2] If the meal will not find its way to the eater, then the eater must find his way to the meal, and further, if the meal is intent upon escaping, then it must not only be sought, but pursued and subjected by strength and skill. There may be traced, in spite of many lapses and exceptions, a general tendency in vital evolution towards increasingly complex bodily organization and increasingly versatile faculties, and *correlated with this advance, a decline in the sufficiency of external instruments to maintain the organism apart from the organism's control.* Improved bodily powers are thus seen, from this viewpoint, to be a kind of compensation for loss of efficiency in the outer series of instruments. Corporeal and external tools, taken together, must in every case be adequate, but the road of evolutionary advance has been for the former to improve as the latter become less and less adequate for the creature's needs. Or, put in another and perhaps a better way, improved bodily structure tends to utilize increasingly intractable material beyond the body. [3]

---

2   Actually, environment and organism change *together;* the external instrument requires more control only as the bodily instrument acquires more ability to exercise that control.
3   The examples which we have taken are drawn, of course, from the Metazoa and Metaphyta, but the same general principle is applicable to the Protista also. It is true that among the latter the power of locomotion does not necessarily accompany a relatively advanced organization. And many multicellular animals of a low grade are mobile. The point which we have been illustrating amounts simply to this—that, whatever faculties an organism has gained in the course of evolution, whether of independent motion or any other, these fulfil a need which is not supplied by environment. It has happened that among the more advanced Metazoa, and among the vertebrates especially, the necessities of obtaining food, of finding a mate and fertilizing her, and sometimes of escaping from enemies, have been met by the development of sense organs of a special kind and locomotor apparatus. Life has devised many other ways of meeting these needs—ways which involve the development of different but nevertheless complex apparatus. The measure of the advance of the organism in all such instances is the measure of the increase of its control over the world.

We come now to a kind of tool that requires of its user something more than the faculties of vision and mobility. The animal that finds and selects an inanimate tool has still to put its tool to use. Here is an instrument in itself worthless, a shiftless inactive object that can only be given effective motion by dint of strenuous exertion, a tool that needs skill and power not its own. Such a tool is in some respects the least tractable of all those that we have considered. It is true, of course, that a flintstone is not a dangerous antagonist, as the prey of the predator may sometimes be, nor does it seek to avoid the world-be user. In these respects the stone implement requires less activity, but in its employment a greater degree of control is necessary and higher faculties are involved. Once the predator has caught and killed his prey all else is easy, but when the suitable stone tool is found, the finder is at once presented with many problems as to its use. The utility of the slain animal is a foregone conclusion to the carnivore, but for the primitive man all will depend upon the skill and intelligence with which he is able to wield his new-found tool. Its value depends far more upon himself than upon the intrinsic qualities of the thing he grasps.

Nevertheless the unfashioned tool is available without any effort save that involved in the finding; it is a provision of nature, no more dependent for its form and constitution upon man than the sunlight is dependent upon the plant. To the fabricator the manufactured tool owes its form as well as its employment. The manufacture of a tool requires a higher degree of intelligence, activity of a still more advanced kind. The tool is at first imperfect, before the flint can be serviceable it must be knapped into the desired form by the skilful workman and activated by the no less skilful craftsman or hunter. The more complex tool, made from several kinds of material brought together from places far apart, shaped in its several parts and assembled, is a more complete creation of the organism's, an altogether new thing, made possible only by the superior faculties of man.

Though the simple tool, once devised and made, does not render strenuous action on the part of its employer unnecessary, sometimes it lightens his old tasks. But perhaps as frequently it makes for increased industry. New artificial weapons make it possible to attack dangerous animals that before had been avoided at all costs. Keener implements allow the building of bigger and more intricate structures. Larger boats enable men to venture further afield. Heavier swords and stronger bows require mightier arms. But when the motive power behind the tool is removed from the user to an artificial energy-providing device, man's role has commenced to decline. At first, active supervision and assistance are required, but gradually the machine is endowed with powers of auto-adjustment and the man becomes little more than a passive spectator. Here lies the turning point in the history of man's works. Up to this point artifice has demanded more and more from man; beyond it, artifice begins to require less from him. The peak has been gained. What of the other side?

We have seen how, even at the present time, many men are enveloped within an intricate system of artificial organs which operate with little need for effort on the part of the user, and we have considered the possibility of a great increase of automatism among these organs. It is not unlikely that some of the bodily organs, which are becoming redundant under these conditions of life, will eventually be diminished or altogether removed, either by artificial selection or direct modification, or possibly by both methods. There is a tendency for man to 'degenerate' physically, to lose the use of faculties and organs which, like some of those which once belonged to the typical parasite, have now become useless in the new environment. As the plant has all that it needs for life brought, as it were, to its own doorstep, so has our well-to-do man of the future, and so, to a less extent, have some men today. As the plant has no need to make up for any shortcomings in the working of its exterior instruments, so man is becoming freed from the toiling and spinning of life. That condition which always attends the improvement of physical faculties and of bodily organs—namely, the use of external instruments which need first to be changed, or contended with, or made, before they can become of use, is here no longer to be found. Accordingly, a certain decline in bodily organization and faculties is to be expected.

There is one human activity, however, which makes for the preservation of the older body and its functions. Play, exercise for its own sake or deliberately in order to maintain health—these seem at present to be increasing rather than otherwise. Perhaps for a long time such substitutes for labour and hunting and fighting will succeed in maintaining the body unimpaired by its easy environment. But it is no less possible that, if human endeavour is to concentrate itself increasingly upon mental and 'spiritual' achievements, physical games will yield place to mental ones. It is probably true that artists and thinkers and scientists are, in the aggregate, less inclined for bodily exertion than the average man; their energy is diverted into other channels. If the human race comes to consist more and more of such people, it may well be that the conservative influence of play will no longer remain. And if it should persist, then there remains the further possibility that it will become partially mechanized, that the energy for the game will be provided by artificial means, and only the directive skill by the players.

We must be careful to note in passing that there is reason to doubt whether changes affecting the body of the organism affect also, to a serious degree, its germ cells. Without accepting or rejecting Weismann's theory, this much is fairly certain: the potential characters of future generations will not be altered rapidly by the acquisition of new 'degenerate' characters in the individual's lifetime. We are not obliged to burn all our bridges behind us. As we have seen, however, artificial selection may be called in to change those potential characters, and, in addition, the environment in which alone those characters might have been realized will have been left far behind.

There seem, then, to be grounds for the belief that one of the effects of tool-using upon man will be what is loosely termed bodily 'degeneration'. He is likely to meet with a fate that is in some important ways like that of Sacculina. The parasite employs its host to see for it, to hunt and travel and feed on its account (if we may put it so), and the man has a no less accommodating host in society.

Within the great 'organism' he tends to become a kind of parasite, and, as some non-human zoologist of the future might say, a most degenerate one at that.

If the body is likely to suffer these changes, will the mind fare likewise? Will the social 'host' take from us also the business of thinking? It seems that many have believed so. In *The Phaedrus*, Plato makes one of his puppets deplore the invention of writing—so long ago did men discern the danger of the artificial. With books at our disposal, the King of Egypt urges, we may well afford to neglect the training of the memory, and what stimulus remains for contemplation? Notions that more diligent and brilliant men have propounded the ordinary man is unlikely to try to work out for himself. He will have recourse to his bookshelves, and will accept naively the conclusions of the thinker. And so he becomes unable to ponder deeply or to remember accurately. The muscles of his mind become atrophied through lack of exercise, whereas without books he would be compelled to rely upon his own powers, however meagre, and to develop them, however slightly, by constant use. Essentially the same objection to the artificial has been posed, under a multitude of forms, by innumerable forms, by a multitude of writers since Plato. In our own time, for example, many protest that, while modern inventions have made competent musical performances audible to large numbers of men, these men are withheld from amateur music of their own making; that in these days of cheap machine-made ornament, craftsment are not likely to spend many days elaborating with care and love simple objects by means of simple tools. That the youth who would otherwise be playing a game of indifferent skill with his friends now goes to watch the accomplished play of professionals; that the radio and the cinema and the novel are fast becoming a substitute for life.

And, as to the future, Mr Lionel Britton, in his play called Brain, gives us a picture of the way in which thinking may possibly be done for us (in so far as one may think for another) by means of a vast and complex organ, a comprehensive repository of information which may be relied upon to tell us quickly what we desire to know upon almost every conceivable subject.

These somewhat melancholy considerations concerning the effects of the improved instrument upon its user appear at first to be at variance with the conclusions of our previous chapter. There we spoke of man as artificializing every field, extending further his understanding and control of himself and his environment, becoming more and more the arbiter of his own fate, continuing in creation. But it was of man in the aggregate that these things were said, and not of the individual. A community needs but a small proportion of really creative individuals within it in order to extend its control over nature. A few inventors, a handful of thinkers, one or two original artists in a generation, are sufficient to impregnate the social mass, to heave the rest forwards—or backwards, according to the way we are facing. The means for spreading knowledge and ideas, and the facilities for making and distributing new articles of use among the members of a community, are now so advanced that a man often lives to see the lives of all changed beyond belief by reason of one creative act of his. We spoke of *man* as the creator of new things, such as, for example, wireless telegraphy. Now, though many workers in the past and a number of contemporary ones have contributed to the result, yet those men who have had nothing to do with the invention, or with the necessary steps towards it, are in an overwhelming majority. It is given to most men to receive the gifts of creators and render little of their own in return. The great creators are abnormal, but upon such does the advance of the artificial depend.

Society is a most fruitful field, in which the seeds of new things seldom fail to grow and flourish exceedingly. No doubt if the season is unkind and the soil unprepared, good germs perish; but many more, even if they have to lie dormant until the conditions for growth are realized, yield at last a full crop. Not only does the social environment lend itself to the dissemination of new notions and material works, but also to their growth, to the progressive accumulation of small fragments of new material derived from many sources. Every year sees the growth of science and technical constructions to more impressive dimensions, not by any means because of any virtue of ours, but because we commence where the last generation laid down its tools. If there should ever arise a generation that created nothing of note whatever, yet they would undoubtedly point with pride to the fine structure of their forefathers' making, and some of them would try to pass it off as their own. It would belong to them only in the sense in which the host belongs to the parasite, the field to the flower, the man to the garment. You can truly own the work of the past only by creating from yourself what advances beyond your initial inheritance. It is fatally easy to argue from community to individual, to shift the qualities of social wholes onto the units that comprise them. This error, more than any other, has been responsible for the confusion of thought which leads some to talk always of human progress and others only of decline. The power of a society, the degree of control which society exercises over its environment—these are no true criteria of the power of the individual or of his dominion over his world.

It is characteristic of life in human society that the individual shall set out, not from some primitive starting point, but from a position somewhat in advance of previous starters. Only so can accumulation occur. A great part of the race that our fathers have run we have to take for granted. We may survey their struggles and failings and successes and take some account of the country through which they have come, but it is not for us to retravel that path. This that they have done, this contest that they have won, is over; it is given, become *natural*. Their score has been recorded. We inherit their prizes, but we cannot inherit the exhilaration of their triumph or the trained muscles that won the victory. There is yet another lap to be run, and over another stretch of ground. There are prizes of our own to be won and muscles of our own to be strengthened. But at this point our metaphor will serve no longer. For what our fathers have done has made our part either more difficult, or, if we so choose, easier. More difficult, because to add new knowledge we must master much of the great body of information which they have gathered; easier because their achievements have left us with artificial means of livelihood which invite laziness. The standards for successful effort have been set high. There is reason for discouragement, and it is indeed fatally easy to retire from the arduous life of creativeness, to settle down to a comfortable and parasitic existence.

Plato's warning is not to be set aside with contempt, nor are the writings of our modern pessimists. The dangers that we face—in which we are even now involved—are very real ones. To us much is given, of us shall be much required. To the extent that our books inform without stimulating thought, or entertain without inspiring, to the extent that works of art allay rather than excite our urge to create, and pursuits of an 'academic' nature take the place of constructive work—by so much do we tend to become mere parasites, to surrender individuality, to yield to the shaping power of exterior forces instead of shaping ourselves. The questions which we have to face are: am I content with my instruments, do they lack nothing that I can give them; are the means of life beyond my body adequate without need for effort of mine—save perhaps the slight effort of choice—to make them more so; have I nothing to contribute to the world of thought and artistic endeavour? The plant and the thorough-going parasite interfere with the working of their external instruments very little; these are, from their users' viewpoint, nearly automatic. All loss of individuality and retrogression come, not so much of difficult conditions or easy conditions merely, as of increased reliance upon what is beyond the creature. All progress is correlated with insufficient external instruments, with a 'nature' that needs control. Progress is progress in power, in control over

247

environment, and control is not exercised over material that it cannot affect. If we feel our mental or physical environment to be imperfect and take what steps we can to improve it, then we are creative, our individuality is enhanced; if we feel that intervention is unnecessary, that we can contribute nothing, then we come perilously near to the parasitic condition. If the display of past human achievement is no spur to effort, but only a discouraging exhibition of what we can never hope to improve, then it would perhaps be well for us if we were without such a heritage.

Though we cannot conclude, from an examination of the creativeness of the community as a whole, the condition of the average individual within it, all advance in the control of a society of its environment is due, of course, to the creativeness of some of its individuals. These are the men who, by extending our control over nature, by helping to improve the instruments of our bodies and minds, make further extension and further improvement more difficult. But we need have little fear that eventually science will have no more to discover, that thought will have made every possible construction out of facts, that instruments will become efficient beyond the possibility of further improvement. There is very little ground for satisfaction with our achievements to date, and there is all too much reason for discontent. Conflict is essential for creation. If ever there should come a time when all men become complacent, such a condition would not indicate that nothing remains for them to do; rather it would show that the *élan* (or whatever you choose to call the unknown vital urge) has died down in them. For such a malady who will find a cure?

One of the tasks of the individual, and it is no easy one, is to keep pace with advances, not in every field—for that would be impossible, but to furnish himself with enough knowledge to make possible a critical and intelligent attitude to human affairs. Specialization in some direction is no doubt useful to him for this purpose, as well as to society for other purposes. But the business of keeping abreast of the more important results of modern endeavour is becoming increasingly difficult. Even Aristotle could not now take all knowledge as his province. It will probably be found necessary, if mere learning on one hand or mere criticism without information on the other are not to crowd out constructive thinking, to revise drastically the kind of 'education' which we now enjoy or suffer, to prune it of unessentials, to encourage a more original outlook that is at the same time a more informed one, and greatly to extend the period of school and university training. Our problem is to steer ourselves carefully between brutal ignorance and knowledge so tightly packed that it can assume no recognizable or original shape.

The danger which we are considering threatens not so much the man of marked individuality (he has other dangers) as the man-in-the-street, the citizen who is for the most part content with current prejudices, him whom some writers love to call 'a mere cog in the machine'. No doubt the capacities of this common man are underrated by many. No one can escape some measure of creativeness, and further, creativeness may be drawn out by an appropriate kind of education and by supplying a milieu favourable to its expression. Leisure from toil that is socially necessary is almost bound to increase. Monotonous labour that gives little or no scope for fresh method and result is almost bound to decline, yielding opportunity for creation, for self-imposed and self-directed tasks. But auspicious conditions need individuals that are able to use them to the full.

We are brought back, then, to the need for remaking man, for producing an individual that will be able to thrive in his new efficient environment, one that will find in the modern conditions a stimulant instead of a soporific. Up to the moment the greater part of human endeavour has been devoted to the improvement of exterior conditions. What of the individual for whom these conditions are created? He has neglected himself. He has fallen behind the instruments that he—or rather the race—has put in motion. It is now his turn to regain the space which he has allowed to grow between himself and them. Once his tools get beyond his control he is in danger. Having artificialized so completely his environment, he must now begin to artificialize himself. The creativeness of the few demands a measure of creativeness from the many. Artifice itself continually brings about a situation that demands more and more artifice, or leads inevitably to stagnation. No one can be quite certain which of these two paths man is about to take.

In any case, all trace of 'parasitism' cannot be avoided. If men are to devote their lives largely to advanced mental and 'spiritual' pursuits, to the ends of life, then automatic means of life will be welcomed. Bodily dependence, with its accompaniment of physical modification, or 'degeneration', will be acceptable. This much—the artificial body—is, for the time being and for some men, given. More practical-minded persons may see to it. The speculative thinker, the scientist, and the artist are content to exercise their creative gifts in other directions. They are willing to accept the benefits of what the practical man has in control. And likewise the practical man will probably be content to accept from the others the major results of their labours without over-particular examination. Specialization is one of the conditions of society, and division of labour is nothing but a pleasant name for a condition that often comes near to a kind of parasitism. In a modern society great dependence in some respects is essential for great independence in others.

What really matters for man is not that he should try to avoid all reliance upon external things, for that is neither possible nor to be desired, nor is it that all men should be creative along similar lines. It is that somewhere or other in the life of each individual there should be strife, that at some point he should find himself confronted with an aspect of 'nature' that he desires above all else to change, to impress with his own mark, to make his own. So has all progress of living forms come about—by struggle against the natural, by relentless refusal to accept things as they are, in a word, by creation.

CHAPTER X

The Artificial

We are near to the end of our enquiry. Our last task is to try to arrive at a general conception which will embrace and give unity to some of the more scattered conclusions of the earlier chapters.

One thing has appeared at every turn in our examination of the artificial, namely, the dual nature of life, and indeed of all things. Again and again we have seen the individual determining itself and what lies beyond, and, in turn, being determined by the world. Inevitably the chain of causation leads outwards from the living thing to its environment, and inwards from the environment to the creature. Inevitably life has two aspects, of freedom and fate, of self-determination and plasticity. Here we have the conception which will serve to draw together many of the loose threads left in the preceding argument.

Spite of innumerable wanderings and fallings by the way, the main trail of evolution leads towards ever increasing individuality, towards ever more organized activity from within, towards ever more extensive dominion over the world. A mere aggregate of particles, we have seen, has some individuality; its form and behaviour proceed to some extent from itself. The pebble has a degree of individuality, but of a rudimentary kind. It is overwhelmingly at the world's mercy.

The crystal shows a certain advance in the scale; it has a characteristic form; its shape proceeds from within. But between 'dead' forms and the primitive organism there is a great gulf. The living creature is no mere clay in the fingers of chance; its structure and behaviour are maintained by an internal principle of unity; it has the secret of using the world as an instrument of its individuality, of employing the 'slings and arrows of outrageous fortune' to further the uniqueness of its own constitution. And yet, of course, it lies under the necessity to become closely adapted to nature. The parasite submits to a narrower world, a sterner discipline, than the free-living creature. Its constitution is determined by the exigencies of life within its host. The active independent animal, by continually changing its relations to circumstances, becomes relatively free; by reason of its mobility it has the power of choice among instruments. And finally man, most individual of animals, adapts the world to himself. Nature still governs him, but, far more than any other animal, he changes nature, and in so doing draws what was once nature into the sphere of his own organic constitution. He becomes an individual of many diverse parts and faculties; he grows from within outwards, casting his outer organs of life in the mould of his intelligence. Such is the trend of evolution, towards the ever more artificial, towards the ever more self-controlling and world-controlling being.

The activity of the organism has two aspects—the mental and the organic, but there is a tendency for us to lay stress upon one aspect and pass lightly over the other. Thus civilization is sometimes regarded as commensurable only with the organic or material achievements of man, sometimes as commensurable only with his mental or spiritual achievements. In either case, whichever criterion is adopted, civilization is essentially artificial. Those men are more civilized who are more inclined to challenge and to change what exists, whether material things or ideas. The truly civilized man is like an inquisitive and mischievous boy who cannot safely be trusted with anything; he will pull all that he can lay hand on to pieces to see how it works, and when he puts it together again, if ever he does so, there will be a noticeable change in himself, and more in his surroundings.

Let us first consider civilization as material advancement. Man finds around himself tools, buildings, towns, methods of manufacture, and the like. All these have become established parts of his life, familiar to everyone. They are taken for granted; their use has become a habit, *second nature* to him. These instruments and modes of life are always affecting a man; always he is adapting himself to them. Their influence works steadily inwards from the periphery to the core. If man does not shift nimbly he will be hoist with his own petard. If the circumstances which he has created are left to take their own course without his active supervision, then he abandons himself to the mercy of his own inventions. He tends to become the creature of the instruments with which he has surrounded himself, like any parasite dwelling within the animal body. Ever there is this tendency for man to surrender his power to his servants, and the danger grows with the servants' ability. Ever man, even if he is really master, must adapt himself to the instruments that serve him. But the only way for him to avoid, as far as may be, the control exerted by his tools, is to continually assert his influence over them, for if he does not master them they will surely master him. He must preserve the artificiality of his environment by continually changing it for his own ends. Ever the artificial is cooling and crystallizing into the natural, and ever must man, if he is to retain and increase his individuality, create a stir in the things about him lest they shall harden into habitual bonds. He cannot avoid the change that is imposed from without, but he may mitigate it by increasingly powerful responses. If his vigilance falters for a moment, nature tightens her strangle-hold.

But, as we have observed, the external organs are in a sense part of his bodily organization, part of himself as a material whole. His control of these instruments is therefore a kind of self-control. By moulding his tools to his designs man in reality moulds himself. By artifice he must contrive to preserve and further the integrity of this greater constitution of his. It is as though his outer parts were continually threatening to secede from or usurp the central government. He has to conciliate them somewhat, but more and more he has to impose a firm dictatorship. Only so is he able to increase his independence and remain civilized. Only by more and more artifice may the untoward consequences of the artificial be forestalled and prevented.

Mere technical advance, however, is in itself no criterion of civility. The mere addition and control of instruments for preserving life is no worthy end for man, but only a means to far greater ends. A broader definition of civilization, which embraces both the organic and the mental aspects of artificial activity, is needed. Let us term that society most civilized which is most creative of ideas as well as material objects; which is prepared to accept neither physical nor mental constructions as they are, without question; which artificializes every field. Civilization, so understood, is not cumulative. It may mark an ancient society more than a modern one. The gauge of a man's civility is not to be found in the validity of his knowledge, in the 'beauty' of his art, or the efficiency of his tools, but rather in the originality, the newness, the creativeness which these show. If we would judge of a community's civilization we must ask ourselves the questions: Are these men creating what shall be, rather than adjusting themselves to what is? Do they tend to examine all things and alter them if need be, or to accept the technical and artistic and religious conventions of a previous age?

A man preserves his bodily individuality only by continual creation of the new. Similarly, only by imposing his own constructions upon the mental factors that come from without, by contributing to and organizing what is given, can he maintain his individuality as a mind. In common parlance *originality* and *individuality* have nearly the same meaning. The man who thinks and feels most for himself, who is least prepared to conform to the arbitrary dictates of what lies beyond, who creates rather than imitates—him men call an *individual*. And they are right. Such a man has mental integrity. If he learns from others, as indeed he must do, it is to arrive finally at his own conclusions. If he reveres nature it is to put his own constructions upon her, to project his own feelings into her. Whether he is an artist, a philosopher or a scientist, he is original. But you cannot be original and have done with it. You must continue so. For the original or artificial idea, once realized, hardens into the conventional or natural. As soon as the creative effort has taken place, and the idea or work has become objectified, then this has become a part of what is, of nature. But in every case it is a matter of degree. Every man, and indeed every organism, is to some extent creative, original, unique. Every organism, even the lowliest, changes its world from moment to moment.

The artist who faithfully imitates the work of other artists, the Church that, instead of leading men, is dragged at their heels, the political institutions that are badgered and driven, as it were at the point of the bayonet, to bring about the necessary changes—in these more especially we see the outward influences working inwards; here external conditions are dominant. But look for the original artist whose work excites the anger of the traditionalist, for the half-persecuted, half-despised sect that is a real force among men, for the tub-thumpers and agitators proclaiming at the street corner, for the originators in every field—working among these you will find the vital force, the creative impulse of the organism striving against the conditions that confront it, pitting the Nature that lies within against the Nature that lies without. This is the Artificial.

As I conclude, my last thought is that, after all, however civilized and pleasant it is to think about our world, this occupation appears of minor significance beside the grim realities of the present situation. The world is now apparently upon the eve of another war, one that will be made all the more terrible and futile by the very activity which we have been considering—by artifice. But the same activity which has made our weapons so deadly, is capable also of searching within society for the root causes of war, of remoulding the 'natural' organization of the community so that we may beat our swords into ploughshares. A halt and blind artifice is our devil; a swift and discerning artifice may be our saviour. Let us end, then with this message of hope and call to another kind of conflict: By artifice let us overcome the artificial that has become as nature.

www.ingramcontent.com/pod-product-compliance
Lightning Source LLC
Chambersburg PA
CBHW071410090426
42737CB00011B/1421